SpringerBriefs in Business

Andrew R. Thomas

American Shale Energy and the Global Economy

Business and Geopolitical Implications of the Fracking Revolution

 Springer

Andrew R. Thomas
College of Business Administration
Department of Marketing
University of Akron
Akron, OH, USA

ISSN 2191-5482 ISSN 2191-5490 (electronic)
SpringerBriefs in Business
ISBN 978-3-319-89305-1 ISBN 978-3-319-89306-8 (eBook)
https://doi.org/10.1007/978-3-319-89306-8

Library of Congress Control Number: 2018939158

Printed on acid-free paper

This Springer imprint is published by the registered company Springer International Publishing AG part of Springer Nature.
The registered company address is: Gewerbestrasse 11, 6330 Cham, Switzerland

Preface

The intended audience for this book is, specifically, my 400+ students each year and, generally, the thousands of students like them—along with their professors and business leaders—who are each seeking to understand the fundamental business and geopolitical implications of America's shale energy revolution.

At the beginning of my career, I was fortunate to travel the world and see first-hand the impact of energy on the lives of governments, organizations, and individuals. When I became an author and researcher, the importance of energy was always present, as I explored topics such as innovation, global strategy, transportation, and security.

As a professor, my primary audience each day is the graduate and undergraduate business students I have the privilege to teach. Trying to see the world through their eyes has led me to this book.

Before each student lies a four or five or even six-decade-long business career. Many things for them will be exponentially different than the business world I came up in. A lot of things already are…

Going forward, we can be certain that energy will continue to play a critical role in shaping the future: *their* future. It is, ultimately, for these ascending business leaders that this book is written.

Akron, OH, USA   Andrew R. Thomas

Contents

About the Author

Andrew R. Thomas, PhD is Associate Professor of Marketing and International Business at the University of Akron and a member of the Core Faculty at the International School of Management in Paris.

He is bestselling author or editor of 23 books, which recently include

The Customer Trap: How to Avoid the Biggest Mistake in Business

Ethics and Neuromarketing: Implications for Market Research and Business Practice

Global Supply Chain Security

Soft Landing: Airline Industry Strategy, Service, and Safety

The Final Journey of the Saturn V

His book *The Distribution Trap: Keeping Your Innovations From Becoming Commodities* was awarded the Berry-American Marketing Association Prize for the Best Marketing Book of 2010.

Andrew is founding editor-in-chief of the *Journal of Transportation Security,* contributing editor at *Industry Week,* and a regularly featured analyst for media outlets around the world such as BBC, CNBC, Fox News, CNN, and ABC.

Dr. Thomas is a founding member of the National Academy of Sciences Global Supply Chain Security Subcommittee.

A successful global entrepreneur, he has traveled to and conducted business in 120 countries on all seven continents.

No One Saw This Coming

February 24, 2016 was a historic day for business and the global economy. If you were only paying attention to the "news of the day," you might have missed a ground-shaking event. Many folks were likely talking about the Grammy Awards, which were held the night before. For political junkies, the focus was on the quadrennial shouting match that is the Presidential Primary Season. Baseball fans surely were looking forward to Spring Training. Yet, as all of this was unfolding on the glowing screens we constantly seem to stare at, something else much more profound, yet subtle, was going on. That day marked the first time natural gas was exported from the USA in more than 40 years. And, while the words "natural gas" and "exports" don't resonate with most people nearly as much as "Jay Z," "Clinton," "Trump," "Cubs," "Indians," or "Yankees" do, the impact of the USA once again producing and exporting ever-larger amounts of natural gas amounts to a true revolution. In every sense of the word.

I realize that this is a sizeable statement, particularly within the first paragraph of this little book. And, that you could reasonably argue the claim is outsized and merely designed to steal your attention away from possibly more interesting content. There is an element of such truth here. Writers and researchers almost always possess a greater level of passion for their topic than anybody else. To go through the arduous and time-consuming process of reading, writing, editing, rewriting, further reading, and reediting requires infatuation with a subject that can border on obsession. As we read the work of others, one is served best to keep a healthy level of scepticism about the materials the author chooses to review, the language they use, and, most importantly, the conclusions they draw. Having said all this, I remain convinced that after spending several years of reading, thinking, and talking to people smarter than myself on the subject of energy's future, we are now going through a revolution the likes of which we have not seen in our lifetimes.

From a 35,000-foot view, it would appear to even a modest observer that something transformative might be going on. A mere 10 years before America's first natural gas export since the 1970s, consensus held across government and industry

© The Author(s), under exclusive licence to Springer International Publishing AG, part of Springer Nature 2018
A. R. Thomas, *American Shale Energy and the Global Economy*, SpringerBriefs in Business, https://doi.org/10.1007/978-3-319-89306-8_1

that the USA was facing both a significant economic and national security threat from dwindling domestic natural gas reserves, as well as increased dependence on foreign oil imports. "America's addiction to oil," as President George W. Bush called it in his 2006 State of the Union Address, had the American leader urging—pleading—for new domestic sources of energy. It seemed the President was trying in vain to halt what already seemed an unstoppable reality: a movement toward the nation's dependency on others for its energy security and, ultimately, its well-being. In 2009, newly elected Barack Obama's first State of the Union reiterated his predecessor's deep concerns when he warned, "We have known for decades that our survival depends on finding new sources of energy, yet we import more oil today than ever before."

To maintain America's economic standing at home—and provide it with the energy so critically needed—several desperate actions were untaken. The launching of the Iraq War in 2003 was in a large part driven by the pursuit of securing that nation's massive oil reserves. A popular saying of the time accurately described the situation: "The 101st Airborne Division wouldn't have been stationed in Tikrit if Iraq's biggest export was asparagus." The folly of the Iraq War was evidenced by the large loss of life and suffering endured by its victims. Trillions of dollars were wasted in a vain attempt to make Iraq into something it could never be. At home, tens of billions of private dollars were rushed in to construct the infrastructure necessary to *import* liquefied natural gas (LNG) into the United States. While war and instability raged across the Mideast, American energy firms doubled down on their risky investments across that region on the hope—really more like a prayer—that new supplies could be secured there. In a lot of directions that people turned, palpable fears about the future of America's domestic energy security—and the country's future—were being raised.

Yet, by 2015, President Obama could proudly and confidently announce in that year's State of the Union address, "Today, no area holds more promise than our investments in American energy. After years of talking about it, we're finally poised to control our own energy future. We produce more oil at home than we have in 15 years. We produce more natural gas than ever before -- and nearly everyone's energy bill is lower because of it." The President was referring to the fact that somewhere around that time the USA surpassed Russia to become the largest energy-producing nation in the world.

Going forward, the prospects of American energy are brighter than any moment in memory. The International Energy Agency (IEA) is the world's foremost government-led organization on reliable, affordable, and clean energy. It is forecasting an even more dramatic increase in energy production that will transform the USA into the world's largest exporter of LNG by the mid-2020s. And, by the late 2020s, the USA—which only recently lifted its ban on oil exports—will ship more oil to foreign markets than it imports. According to the IEA, this revolution of ever-expanding energy production in the USA is already "reordering international trade flows and challenging incumbent suppliers and business models."[1]

---

[1] International Energy Agency, *World Energy Outlook 2017* (OECD/IEA, 2017). p. 24.

So, what happened? And, how did things change so quickly? I'll try my best to answer those questions in the first portion of this book. I realize, however, that what is most important for you the reader is understanding what these changes mean to you and your organization.

Much of what we hear and read about America's energy revolution is focused on the impact of "longer and lower" energy prices, and, secondarily, opportunities within the domestic energy sector. Each of these is crucial for business people to understand. Yet, the American energy revolution is about much more than this. Companies of all sizes, whether they see it or not, are having new opportunities open up for their products and services as a result of America's new energy bounty. I'm thinking of our manufacturing clients who conduct market research projects through a partnership with MAGNET (Manufacturing Growth Network) in Cleveland and the College of Business Administration at the University of Akron.[2] Here is just one example:

A manufacturer of heat exchangers and pressure vessels, who was originally focusing on foreign markets for new growth opportunities, approached us. After digging into the data, we discovered that there were far better opportunities for them domestically than overseas. They decided to allocate their scarce sales and marketing resources to targeting the burgeoning agricultural chemical sector here in the USA. The results were substantial. They have added several new employees in recent months, and have confirmed orders for the next several years.

I realize this may not be the kind of success story that will garner top headlines in the business press. Nevertheless, for this company, its employees, suppliers, customers, and the community where it resides, this is really big news. And such stories are happening all over America. Our clients' success was tied directly to the far broader trends shaping American energy.

Since the 1980s, America's growing energy *insecurity* was forcing US firms across many industries to reconsider their future. For example, dozens of major fertilizer and pesticide plants in the USA were closing—and production was shifting to nations where natural gas supplies were abundant. This was not a trivial development. The USA, which is the largest agricultural producer in the world, grows and exports more wheat, cotton, soybeans, corn, sugar, and citrus than any nation on Earth. Of course, this largesse also means that America is the biggest consumer of agricultural chemicals.

In addition to its role as the biggest agriculture chemical consumer for decades, the USA was also the world's largest producer and exporter. America's abundant natural gas kept prices relatively low. US dominance seemed assured in that industry. However, as American natural gas supplies dwindled and became more expensive (natural gas liquids are vital for the production of these chemicals), the industry underwent a major shift: away from production in America to other parts of the

---

[2] In 2012, a partnership between MAGNET and the University of Akron's College of Business Administration began to provide market research services to manufacturing firms across Northeastern Ohio. MAGNET is the State of Ohio's Manufacturing Extension Program (MEP) representative.

world where those natural gas liquids were more abundant, and cheaper. This was not dissimilar to the 1990s and early 2000s where American workers were replaced by labor in much lower-wage markets such as Mexico and China. By the early years of the 2000s, the USA still remained the largest consumer of agricultural chemicals. To its detriment, the USA had also become the world's largest *importer.*

Today, the tables have turned: the USA is awash in natural gas and oil. The innovations that have facilitated the extraction of this energy have altered the global landscape. Starting in 2014, there were 17 new "AgChem" plants underway in the USA, with nearly 12 million tons of new capacity and an estimated $85 billion of private investment. Further, almost two-dozen retired plants are also being recommissioned and upgraded. In a remarkable turnaround, the USA is set to once again become the world's leading fertilizer and pesticide producer—and exporter—by 2018. Our client is successfully targeting this new opportunity.

Examples like this one are being replicated across many industrial sectors of the US economy, particularly petrochemicals. In 2012, the USA was still the highest cost producer of petrochemicals in the world. As increasing domestic shale gas supply became available, the USA moved to being one of the lowest-cost producers. As a result, in just 5 short years, by 2017, more than $185 billion in new capital investment had flowed to the construction of new nonagricultural chemical plants and supporting infrastructure.[3] More than half of that capital flow came from overseas investors. Even if the average American is unaware about what is happening at home—beyond their lower energy bills—more and more foreigner investors are wide awake when it comes to the business opportunities opened up by America's energy revolution.

The point here is that a company's market research studies and growth strategy should include the impact of the America's energy revolution in the principal calculus. Failing to do so could result in missing out on some of the best business opportunities in our generation. To turn up the resolution even higher, business leaders should also be exposed to the evolution of drilling and extraction techniques that have enabled this new source of energy to come to the surface. Of course, any discussion around the impact of energy is more than merely in economic terms. Nations are markets and markets are nations. Energy's role in transforming the geopolitical landscape cannot be factored out of the discussion. The emerging globalization of American energy will have far reaching influence. Geopolitical considerations and the restructuring of international relations around American energy will impact global business in a myriad of ways for decades to come.

Let me lay out the basis of the thesis here as simply as possible:

1. Despite popular myths to the contrary, today the USA remains the most dominant economic, political, military, diplomatic, and cultural force in history.

---

[3] American Chemistry Council, "Shale Gas and New U.S. Chemical Industry Investment- $185 billion", December 15, 2017, https://www.americanchemistry.com/Policy/Energy/Shale-Gas/ Infographic-Shale-Gas-and-New-US-Chemical-Industry-Investment.pdf. Accessed January 6, 2017.

2. America will become even more ascendant in the coming decades as she becomes the most dominant energy player in the world.
3. We are only at the very beginning of this shift, as American energy development is in its relative infancy, and is likely to only expand in scope and magnitude going forward.
4. The American energy revolution of today is part of a bigger energy transition; one from Nineteenth Century energy sources—such as horses and steam—to the hydrocarbons (oil, gas, and coal) of today. This energy transition began in earnest during World War 1 and remains with us to the present.
5. The nature of energy transitions is that they are gradual and take place over decades or centuries. The technical and infrastructure imperatives needed to build and sustain an energy transition require massive amounts of investment, attention, and other scarce resources. For this reason, energy transitions throughout human history have been quite rare.
6. The current energy transition driven by hydrocarbons is relatively nascent. Alternative energy sources like wind, solar, and geothermal *will* play an ever-growing role in future developments. However, until critical mass is reached by these substitutes to approximate the investment and infrastructure levels of hydrocarbons today—hydrocarbons will remain the dominant energy sources for decades to come.
7. The implications for business are complex and wide-ranging. Because of American shale energy, business leaders are faced with new promises. And, ignore these at their peril.
8. An ever-stronger United States, enhanced by energy dominance, is already reevaluating its foreign policy objectives in the Twenty-First Century, which is certain to alter to the geopolitical landscape around the world.

The impact on American business surrounding the energy revolution has just started to become visible. The purpose of this book is provide the reader with a baseline understanding of the fundamental transformations that have occurred, are occurring, and may possibly occur in the future as a result of America's shale energy revolution.

This book is *not* a vast technical analysis of the ins and outs of the processes around horizontal drilling and hydraulic fracturing: the innovative processes which have made so much of this possible. Nor is this book a moral argument for or against the expanded use of hydrocarbons.[4] Whether one likes—or doesn't like—fossil fuels is not really pertinent here. We are living in the midst of the Carbon Age,

---

[4]To the Reader: I philosophically believe that the continued use of fossil fuels is both moral and human. From my perspective, fossil fuels are what have made so much of human progress possible in recent years. When fossil fuels are more available and their prices lower, the biggest beneficiaries are poor people. Alex Epstein's *The Moral Case for Fossil Fuels* (Portfolio/Penguin, 2014) is a strong starting point into the discussion around the issue. Nevertheless, it is not my purpose here to try to convince you about the efficacy of fossil fuels. This book is only intended to explain what is going on, how we got here, and what it means going forward when it comes to business and geopolitics.

which surged out of its adolescence during World War 1. If there was ever an opportunity to stop or suspend America's shale energy revolution, it likely would have occurred in the early years of the Obama Administration. By 2009–2010, the Federal Government was finally catching up to the innovations that had rapidly taken place within the energy sector. Political leaders were clear as to what was going on and how things were being done. Still, at the Federal level, where center-left majorities existed in both houses of Congress and the White House, policy makers consciously decided not to do anything to block progress on America's shale energy development—even though they had the opportunity and power to do so.

Moreover, this is not a case for or against any particular kind of energy source. As global poverty rates are predicted to continue their plummet, and prosperity spreads to even more and more of the world's population, it is likely that global energy demand will continue to rise. Add in another 2.4 billion human beings to the current population of 7.6 billion over the next 40 years, and *all* energy sources—including renewables, nuclear, fossil fuels, and others—will need to be harnessed to meet demand.

From a business perspective, America's shale energy revolution—rooted in oil and natural gas—is deep, profound, and getting only more so every day. In areas as wide-ranging as manufacturing, business strategy, international trade, supply chain management, and foreign policy, America's shale energy revolution is rewriting the rules. Chapter 3 of this book will explore, within the context of the new energy realities, the business and geopolitical implications of the American shale energy revolution. Before we can do that, however, it is important to learn about how we got to now. That is what the next chapter of this book is about.

Chapter Highlights

- The Carbon Age burst out of its adolescence during World War 1.
- Supported by its domestic energy prowess and access to foreign oil, the United States rose to global dominance as the undisputed superpower during and after World II.
- The American-created Bretton Woods System bolstered global capitalism, which has underpinned and maintained an unprecedented era of peace and prosperity around the world.
- Global capitalism and its many benefits are intimately tied to a reliable and secure hydrocarbon supply.
- Energy shocks starting in the 1970s raised real doubts about the future of American energy security, the sustainability of American Empire, and, the overall future of global capitalism.
- Early Twenty-First Century innovative developments in energy extraction from shale rock—originating in the USA—coupled with unique characteristics of the American society have altered the global energy landscape.

The Carbon Age Emerges

The manifestation of the United States as *the* main player on the global stage has paralleled the evolution of the Carbon Age. Prior to World War I, the primary sources for energy were wood, hydropower, steam, horses, and some coal. As The Great War commenced in 1914, oil remained mostly an afterthought in most planners' minds. There was an overabundance of it. Nevertheless, by 1919, when the Armistice was finally signed, things had changed inexorably. Oil was now

© The Author(s), under exclusive licence to Springer International Publishing AG, part of Springer Nature 2018
A. R. Thomas, *American Shale Energy and the Global Economy,* SpringerBriefs in Business, https://doi.org/10.1007/978-3-319-89306-8_2

recognized as a vital necessity for national survival. Oil had become, in the elegant prose of the economist Julian Simon, "the master, or ultimate, resource."[1]

Experience during World War I educated leaders around the world that the future of their nations—and any other nation-- would be incalculably shaped by its ability to secure oil. Increasingly mechanized armies and navies—airplanes, tanks, trucks, ambulances, other road vehicles, and, most importantly, ocean vessels—all operated on oil. A fleet of 827 motor cars and 15 motorcycles supported the British Expeditionary Force that went to France in 1914. By War's end, November 1918, the British army included more than 56,000 trucks, 23,000 motorcars, and 34,000 motorcycles, all powered by petroleum.[2] Moreover, military aviation had burst on the scene to become the third dimension of warfare: after land and sea. Over the course of the last 2 years of the War, Britain produced and deployed 55,000 planes; France, 68,0000 planes; Italy, 20,000; the USA, 15,000; and Germany, 48,000.[3]

By 1917, petroleum shortages were being experienced on all sides. Oil's availability now moved to the forefront of all military planning. The Interallied Petroleum Conference was established on recommendation of the Interallied Conference at Paris in November. It consisted of representatives from the United States, Great Britain, France, and Italy. Preliminary meetings were held at London as early as February 1918. The first formal meeting was delayed until May 6, 1918, when representatives from the United States could attend. The five sessions held during the war were at Paris, London, and Rome. Several subcommittees dealt with the following subjects: petroleum storage in France; standardization of petroleum products; an importation program in accordance with the schedule of the Allied Maritime Transport Council; and, petroleum requirements of the Allies in Europe and the Mediterranean.[4] The Committee's overall function was to agree upon the petroleum requirements of each Ally; the best sources of supply; and, specifications, tonnage, and routes for conveyance of oil supplies.[5]

By War's end, a new reality existed: Oil had become a dominant force in shaping the operations and conduct of nations. This may have been best articulated by M. Henri Berenger, a French senator, industrialist, and writer, who served as his country's wartime Oil Commissioner and, later, was France's Ambassador to Washington: "He who owns the oil will own the world, for he will rule the sea by means of the heavy oils, the air by means of the ultra refined oils, and the land by means of petrol and the illuminating oils. And, in addition to these, he will rule his fellow men in an economic sense, by reason of the fantastic wealth he will derive from oil—the wonderful substance which is more sought after and more precious today than gold itself."[6] Berenger's comments were more prescient than even he

---

[1] Julian L. Simon *The Ultimate Resource* (Princeton University Press, 1981), p. 162.

[2] Brian C. Black "How World War I Ushered in a Century of Oil", *The Conversation*, April 3, 2017, http://theconversation.com/how-world-war-i-ushered-in-the-century-of-oil-74585   accessed January 2, 2018.

[3] Ibid.

[4] Ronald W. Ferrier *The History of the British Petroleum Company: Volume 1, The Developing Years, 1901-1932* (Cambridge University Press, 1982) p. 356.

[5] John Weaver Frey, H. Chandler Ide, Eds. *A history of the Petroleum Administration for War, 1941-1945* (U.S. G.P.O., 1946), p. 8.

[6] Timothy C. Winegard *The First World Oil War* (University of Toronto Press, 2016), p. 242.

must have realized at the time. World War 1 was an inflection point. Prior to it, the movement of men and materiele was accomplished by Nineteenth Century means. During and immediately after the War, it became abundantly clear that oil had become the nurturing and sustaining resource for all nations.

The War marked the beginning of a large-scale *energy transition*, which, according to Vaclav Smil, is a "gradual shift from a specific pattern of energy provision to a new state of an energy system."[7] Such energy transitions are not to be taken lightly. The scope and magnitude of the fundamentals needed to develop the technical and infrastructural imperatives of an energy transition are enormous. There also exist abundant—and often unintended—social, political, and economic consequences during an energy transition that unfold, materialize, and, finally, need to be dealt with. Energy transitions are, therefore, protracted affairs, which take decades, not years, to be realized.[8]

Of course, oil had been used in a wide variety of ways for centuries prior to World War I. The Scriptures tell us of "oil out of flinty rock" (Deuteronomy 32:13) and "the rock poured me out rivers of oil" (Job 29:6). Dioscorides Pedanius, the Greek historian, detailed how the citizens of Agrigentum, in Sicily, burned oil in lamps prior to the birth of Christ. The ancient Egyptians used oil to prepare mummies, which were burned millennia later to operate locomotives across North Africa.[9] Nonetheless, new demands—first emanating from early Twentieth Century military necessity, and later, from consumer-driven needs—accelerated the energy transition to oil and other carbon energy sources. It is this same energy transition that we are living through today.

The first oil well in America was drilled in 1859. Seventy years later, in 1919, following the Great War, one of the most popular business books in the country could state without hyperbole,

> Petroleum is the fuel and lubricant of speed and mechanical efficiency- on land, on the sea, under the seas, in the air. Practically every human activity is dependent upon it to some degree. But is it is only in the past decade that petroleum has really come into its own. This period has seen the perfection of the internal combustion engine, upon which the automobile, the aeroplane, the farm tractor, motor boats, the submarine, and many other efficient mechanical contrivances depend. Likewise, it has seen the beginning of an era of fuel oil for railway and marine transportation... Oil is now the new *monarch of motion*.[10]

At the same time, fears—real or imagined—had convinced many that "peak oil" had been reached; that supply was soon to run out if new sources couldn't be found. Skyrocketing demand for oil during and immediately after the War left many wondering how long existing oil supplies could last.

---

[7] Vaclav Smil *Energy Transitions: History, Requirements, Prospects* (Praeger, 2010), p. vii.

[8] Ibid., p. viii.

[9] John James McLaurin Sketches in *Crude Oil: Some Accidents and Incidents of the Petroleum Development in All Parts of the Globe* (Publisher: Author, 1896), p. 5.

[10] Reid Sayers McBeth *Oil: The New Monarch of Motion* (Markets Publishing Corp., 1919), p. 1.

Global oil production before and during the War was overwhelmingly an American affair, with the USA accounting for more than 70% of all global output by 1918. Moreover, during the War, the USA provided over 90% of all the oil to the Allied Nations.

Total global oil production 1913–1918 (in '000 tons)[11]

Country	1913	1914	1915	1916	1917	1918
Russia	9200	8900	9100	8700	8600	3700
USA	34,000	36,400	38,500	41,200	45400	48,800
Austria-Hungary	1100	900	700	900	900	800
British India	1200	1100	1200	1200	1200	1200
Romania	1800	1800	1600	900	700	100
Mexico	3800	3900	4900	6100	8300	9500
Other countries	2900	3300	3500	3800	4500	4900
World total	54,000	56,300	59,500	62,800	69,600	68,900

Early on, the Americans recognized the significance of oil both during the War and its aftermath. Most of the other warring parties realized later that motor vehicles and fuel would become critical factors of military and, therefore, national importance. They neither established strategic oil reserves before August 1914, nor did they make serious efforts to raise the oil production in their own area of influence during the War.[12] As the War ended, it was the Americans, followed later by everyone else, who led the scramble to find more oil.

Despite the fact that the USA was by far the biggest oil-producing nation in the world, domestic demand was rising much faster than supply. While exports to the Allies during the War consumed larger and larger quantities of US production, developments on the home front further placed huge expectations on domestic supply. The unprecedented mobilization that characterized America's entry into the War saw investment in new manufacturing and equipment more than quadruple: from $600 million in 1915 to $2.5 billion in 1918.[13]

By the end of the War, both business and consumers were eager to refocus. General Motors, for example, reported the number of cars, trucks, and tractors it sold for the first quarter in 1920 had risen 45.2% over the previous year.[14] General Motors' incredible growth was reflected in the broader automotive industry. Auto sales in America had quadrupled from 1909 to 1913, and then quadrupled again from 1913 to 1920. Americans bought 3.6 million cars in 1923, and by the end of the roaring 1920s, Americans owned 23 million private cars, out of a total population of 124 million people. In 1921, there were 387,000 miles of paved roads in the

---

[11] Ferdinand Friedensburg *Das Erdöl im Weltkrieg*, Stuttgart 1939, p. 121.

[12] Gliech, Oliver: "Petroleum: 1914–1918-online". *International Encyclopedia of the First World War*, ed. by Ute Daniel, Peter Gatrell, Oliver Janz, Heather Jones, Jennifer Keene, Alan Kramer, and Bill Nasson, issued by Freie Universität Berlin, Berlin 2015-01-07. https://encyclopedia.1914-1918-online.net/article/petroleum accessed January 3, 2018.

[13] William Pelfrey *Billy, Alfred and, General Motors: The Story of Two Unique Men, a Legendary Company, and a Remarkable Time in American History* (AMACOM, 2006), p. 6.

[14] Ibid.

country. By 1929, there were 687,000 miles.[15] The "Monarch of Motion" was now evident for all to see. American energy companies responded to the demand by lots of new drilling. Between 1915 and 1920, the number of wells drilled across the country increased to almost 34,000 and oil production soared by roughly 45%.[16] It is not hype to say that The Great War and the rise of an oil-centric economy transformed the USA. It would also be accurate to note that the War forced a penetrating reevaluation on how America would interact with the other nations of the world.

Oil and the Interwar Years

After the Allied triumph over the Central Powers, America's position relative to other nations remained uncertain. As Ed Conway notes, America before the War was a "bit player" on the global stage relative to the other major powers.[17] Indeed, while America had passed Britain to become the world's largest economy sometime during the 1890s, US geopolitical influence and interest remained limited primarily to the Western Hemisphere and the South Pacific.

The Americans finally jumped into the European conflagration with a Declaration of War on April 2, 1917. Woodrow Wilson, who had been re-elected a mere 5 months before on the slogan "At least he kept us out of war," orchestrated this leap into the European conflict. The 180-degree turn by Wilson and the events that followed sent shockwaves throughout the nation. At the time of its entry into the conflict, the US Army had only 200,000 active soldiers, of which 80,000 were National Guardsmen. The ranks would have to be expanded immediately. This was done through volunteer enlistments and conscription. The passage of the Selective Service Act in 1917 led to the registration of more than 24 million men to become eligible for the draft. Over the next 18 months (April 1917–November 1918), more than four million men served in the American Expeditionary Force, while another 600,000 served in the US Navy and 78,000 in the Marine Corps. In this relatively short period of time, 116,516 American service personnel were killed and 204,002 wounded.[18] As a point of reference, in the Vietnam War, which lasted from 1964 to 1973, more than 8.7 million Americans served in the armed forces. 58,220 military personnel were killed and 153,303 wounded.[19] Further, the total population of the USA in 1918 was 103.2 million; by 1973 it had more than doubled to 212 million. In short, World War I was a quick, yet bloody experience for the Americans.[20]

---

[15] Edmund Clingan *Capitalism: A Modern Economic History* (iUniverse, 2015), p. 313.

[16] Robert McNally *Crude Volatility: The History and the Future of Boom-Bust Oil Prices* (Columbia University Press, 2017), p. 53.

[17] Ed Conway *The Summit Bretton Woods, 1944: J.M. Keynes and the Reshaping of the Global Economy* (Pegasus Books, 2014), p. 39.

[18] Nese F. DeBruyne "American War and Military Operations: Lists and Casualties" *Congressional Research Service*, April 26, 2017, p. 2. https://fas.org/sgp/crs/natsec/RL32492.pdf. Accessed January 8, 2018.

[19] Ibid.

[20] U.S. Census Bureau, "History of the U.S. Population" https://census.gov/topics/population.html. Accessed January 8, 2018.

The scale and rapidity of death on the fields of France stunned many Americans. It quickly turned them sour on war in general, and, later, their leadership and the European Allies. President Wilson, on the other hand, sought to use the shocking brutality of the War to pedal an idealism grounded in international conflict resolution. Seeking to re-brand the conflict as "The War to End All Wars," Wilson poured all of his energies into establishing The League of Nations. After more than 6 months of negotiations in Europe, Wilson returned home in 1919 to see his future vision come crashing down. The American people—reeling from the bloodletting of their sons, brothers, and husbands—couldn't accept Wilson's overambitious, idealistic vision. Americans turned their backs on Europe's long history of self-destruction. Congress never ratified American participation in the League; and, US interest in the political affairs of Europe evaporated away.

This is not to say, however, that the USA withdrew back to its prewar isolationism. Quite to the contrary, America's coming of age as a superpower was now underway. The War saw to that. In 1914, the US Dollar was quoted in fewer financial centers than the Italian Lira or Austrian Schilling.[21] London was the undisputed capital global financial hub, responsible for more than half of the entire world's exported capital, and financing most of the flow of international trade.[22] By 1919, Britain, in order to maintain its war effort, had liquidated 15 percent of all of its overseas investments, most of it to the USA Also during the War, Britain and the other Allies also ran up tremendous debts to the US government, who had extended generous loans that eventually totaled $7 billion.[23] And, in addition to the overwhelming majority of oil that America provided the Allies during the war, the USA also became the "factory and granary" to the world. American machinery and foodstuffs were shipped in ever-bigger quantities to the four corners of the world.[24] By the mid-1920s, the torch had been passed. The dominant currency in the world was now the US Dollar, having replaced British Sterling. The center of gravity of international trade and finance was now firmly in America.

Like its economy, American foreign policy was stimulated by the War, yet in a different direction. The focus wasn't so much on "Mother Europe." Instead it was on places where oil could be located and extracted: Oil that had quickly become the mother's milk of the American—and global—economy. The Monarch of Motion was now to significantly shape the course of US foreign policy.

Amounting to almost an obsession, American political and business leaders embarked on a global quest together after the War in search for overseas oil. It led them first to Mesopotamia, Mexico, Venezuela, the Dutch East Indies, Colombia,

---

[21] Barry Eichengreen *Exorbiant Privilege: The Rise and Fall of the Dollar and the Future of the International Monetary System* (Oxford University Press, 2011), p. 32.

[22] Conway, *The Summit Bretton Woods, 1944: J.M. Keynes and the Reshaping of the Global Economy*, p. 40.

[23] Ibid.

[24] Eichengreen *Exorbiant Privilege: The Rise and Fall of the Dollar and the Future of the International Monetary System*, p. 32.

and Peru. As American diplomats were not highly specialized in regions outside of the Western Hemisphere, the pursuit for overseas oil didn't go well at first. The more experienced British and French in the Middle East and Sumatra outmaneuvered the Americans. In Mexico and South America, the USA did fare better, primarily due to its longstanding presence there. Meanwhile, vast new discoveries in California, Texas, and Oklahoma, coupled with the fresh supply from the Western Hemisphere, abated the threat of oil scarcity, and by 1924 a surplus had been created.[25]

Despite the passing of the immediate storm, President Calvin Coolidge remained concerned that the surplus would only be temporary. He was clear in his belief that excessive oil production by private companies could only lead to future shortages and oil-driven crises.[26] In short, the private sector could not be trusted. The hand of government was needed to smooth over any rough patches and ensure oil's uninterrupted flow. Coolidge warned that the US government would not stand idly by since "the supremacy of nations may be determined by the possession of available petroleum and its products."[27] From Coolidge's point of view, national considerations around oil were beginning to trump the interests of the private sector. Coolidge was particularly concerned about rising military requirements, with priorities on oil procurement for naval vessels, and the burgeoning air force. Further, oil had already become one of the nation's most vibrant and profitable industries, and was a major contributor to the overall health and stability of the American economy.[28]

In the decades after World War I, the most significant development in American oil policy—and, ultimately, the nation's foreign policy—was the entanglement of businessmen and government officials working to meet *both* the nation's strategic objectives and industry's goals. As we'll see shortly, this spider's web of interests, factions, and characters eventually coalesced toward the common goal of sustaining and expanding global capitalism. It is the distinctive feature of American Empire. The interworking between government and industry has remained a fundamental characteristic of the American way of doing things. In short, the American government has played an exceptional role in launching the modern global capitalism system; and, the government continues to influence much of its management today.[29] And, it would often be oil that served as the lubricant that would reduce the natural friction between the American government and American business to make global capitalism possible.

---

[25] Gerald D. Nash *United States Oil Policy, 1890-1964: Business and Government in Twentieth Century America* (University of Pittsburgh Press Digital, 1968), p. 49.

[26] McNally *Crude Volatility: The History and the Future of Boom-Bust Oil Prices*, p. 56.

[27] Norman Nordhauser "Origins of Federal Oil Regulations in the 1920's" *Business History Review* 47:1 (1973) p. 19.

[28] Nash *United States Oil Policy, 1890-1964: Business and Government in Twentieth Century America*, p. 73.

[29] Sam Gindin and Leo Panitch *The Making of Global Capitalism: The Political Economy Of American Empire* (Verso Books, 2012), p. 1.

For Americans, government and industry agreed that increasing the presence of US companies in foreign oil fields was a mutual interest. Not only was foreign oil usually cheaper to produce (which served business' objectives by boosting company profits), utilizing overseas oil to meet foreign demand reduced the potential drain on US reserves (a stated national goal of the government). The Americans, undeterred from British domination of the Middle East in the 1920s, continued to look for ways to penetrate what was quickly becoming one of the most important regions in the world. It seemed there were only two ways for American firms to break the stronghold of the British in the region: either acquire access to Britain's exclusive Iraq Petroleum Company (IPC), which held the bulk of the oil concessions in the States of the former Ottoman Empire (which included present-day Iraq, Saudi Arabia, Turkey, and the adjoining sheikdoms); or, proceed independently, outside of the IPC framework, which included present-day Iran, Kuwait, Israel, and Jordan.[30]

The US government supported a two-pronged approach for American companies to seek entry into the Middle East while avoiding a clash with Britain. The first approach involved a State Department effort to negotiate on behalf of US oil companies the right to purchase access to the IPC's holdings. After arduous back and forths—many involving the highest levels of the US and British governments—the IPC opened its doors to Standard Oil of New Jersey and Socony-Vacuum Oil Company (which later became Mobil). In 1929, the two American firms were granted a combined 23.75 share of IPC.[31]

The second approach into the Middle East focused on the US government supporting efforts by other US oil companies to gain concessions in the region outside of the area held by the IPC. In 1930, Standard Oil of California (SOCAL) obtained a concession on the island of Bahrain, off the coast of Saudi Arabia. In 1933, SOCAL obtained extensive concession rights in Saudi Arabia. The Texas Company joined forces with SOCAL in Bahrain and Saudi Arabia in 1936. Meanwhile, Gulf Oil Company, in partnership with Anglo-Persian, had gained access to Kuwait.[32] In each of these cases, government support was critical in "opening the door" for the oil companies to establish relationships with the responsible leaders in the region. In Rachel Bronson's phrase, the American leap into the Middle East during the 1920s and 1930s "set the stage for the next 50 years".[33]

It is critical to recall that while the USA actively pursued—and secured—foreign sources of oil supply in the Interwar Years, American domestic supply was dramatically increased as well. For example, by 1930, the East Texas Oilfield had been brought online. Since then, some 30,340 wells have been drilled within its 140,000 acres to yield nearly 5.2 billion barrels of oil: America's largest domestic energy

---

[30] Rachel Bronstein *Thicker Than Oil: America's Uneasy Partnership with Saudi Arabia* (Oxford University Press, 2006), p. 16.

[31] Ibid.

[32] Ibid., p. 17.

[33] Ibid., p. 35.

find ever.[34] Huge finds like this one, and others in California and Oklahoma, melded with the new acquisitions in the Western Hemisphere and Middle East, and gave the USA oil supremacy over most of the rest of the world. By 1930, it seemed America's long national goal of energy security had finally been accomplished.

Yet, all the while, the rise in ever-larger supplies, and the financial and economic collapse that marked the Great Depression, threatened to destroy everything. By 1933, prices in some areas of the country had reached 4 cents *a barrel*! This was not 4 cents a gallon, but 4 cents a barrel. For reference, oil has been measured in barrels since 1866, when independent drillers met in Titusville Pennsylvania to standardize the size of a barrel of petroleum. Since then, a barrel is measured as 42 gallons of crude oil. It is the global standard used by everyone. Today, in the USA, the typical 42-gallon barrel's refined products include about 20 gallons of gasoline, 12 gallons of diesel, and 4 gallons of jet fuel and other products like liquefied petroleum gases and asphalt. Again, by 1933, the price of a barrel of crude oil in some places had plummeted to 4 cents.[35] The industry was in chaos and America's oil advantage appeared to be disappearing.

Leaders across the oil industry and government were clamoring for the Roosevelt Administration to do something to stave off a full-blown destruction. On May 5, 1933, Harold Ickes, the Secretary of the Interior, was handed a telegram from the Governor of Texas saying, "The situation is beyond the control of the state authorities." Three days later, Ickes warned that "the oil business has about broken down and to continue to do nothing will result in the utter collapse of the industry."[36] Ickes, a lawyer by trade and no friend of the big business practices of the energy giants, spoke for more than himself when he observed, "There is no doubt about our absolute and complete dependence upon oil. We have passed from the Stone Age, to bronze, to iron, to the industrial age, and now to an age of oil. Without oil, American civilization as we know it could not exist."[37]

As had been the case in the past—and would be in the future—the American government would use its power to ensure a stable oil supply. In simple terms, Washington's response to this energy crisis was the creation of a regulatory regime that set floors on oil prices and ceilings on oil imports. And, it worked. By the end of the 1930s, American oil production and prices had fully stabilized.

World War II, Bretton Woods, and American Ascendancy

It was World War II that finally launched the USA to pinnacles of power never seen before in human history. Even prior to its entry into the war in 1941, America possessed the world's largest economy; enjoyed the fruits of the Dollar as the premiere

---

[34] Julia Cauble Smith, *Handbook of Texas Online*, "East Texas Oilfield," Accessed January 15, 2018, http://www.tshaonline.org/handbook/online/articles/doe01.

[35] Daniel Yergin *The Prize: The Epic Quest for Oil, Money, and Power* (Free Press, 2008) p. 237.

[36] Ibid.

[37] Ibid.

currency of international trade; contained the globe's financial and trade center, and, produced and exported more oil than any other nation. America's further rise during the War would make it a superpower without challenge, and one that remains so to the present. Frankly, any discussion around American "decline" in the present day is laughable and childish.

During the War, American oil production amounted in all to six billion barrels, out of the total of seven billion barrels, consumed by the Allies during the conflict. This fueled an unmatched military buildup in world history. Between 1940 and 1945, the American Navy added 6,700 new ships, of which 124 were aircraft carriers. The Merchant Marine added 34 million tons of new ocean cargo vessels. For the Army Air Corps and Navy, 324,000 aircraft were produced, including the War's most expensive single item: the B-29 Bomber. On the ground, the US Army and Marines Corps received 110,000 tanks, and 2.4 million other military vehicles including military jeeps and trucks. All the while the Manhattan Project harnessed atomic energy and developed nuclear weapons.[38] President Roosevelt named Harold Ickes as Petroleum Coordinator for National Defense. During the war, Ickes worked closely with industry executives to oversee a 30% expansion in total oil production in the United States. This increase enabled the Allies to secure the final push and achieve complete victory over Germany and Japan.[39]

By the end of World War II, the United States had emerged as more than just an economic superpower. Its military might was unequaled. The US Navy reigned supreme on the seas and was the mightiest fleet ever to sail. America's aircraft patrolled the skies without any interference. Also, the nation had already shown both the capacity to build a nuclear weapon and, equally important, the will to use it. More than half of all the capital on planet Earth was in American hands. No country in history was ever so powerful. It is so today.

The simmering question for many leaders around the world was "What would America do with all of this power in its hands?" Much of the answer could be found in an essay written by Henry Luce just prior to America's entry into the war. It was entitled *The American Century*. Luce was no ordinary Amercian citizen. He was probably one of the most influential private citizens in the America of his day.[40] Luce's hold on American opinion cannot be overstated. A media magnate in the pre-television era, Luce's collection of publications were regularly read by tens of millions of Amercians. *Time* summarized and interpreted the week's news. *Life* was a picture magazine of politics, culture, and society that dominated American visual perceptions. *Fortune* explored in-depth the economy and the world of business. *Sports Illustrated* explored the motivations and strategies of sports teams and key

---

[38] Threse numbers were aggregated from Ian V Hogg The American Arsenal: The World War II Official Standard Ordnance Catalogue (Frontline Books, 2014).

[39] McNally *Crude Volatility: The History and the Future of Boom-Bust Oil Prices*, p. 92.

[40] Robert Edwin Herzstein *Henry R. Luce, Time, and the American Crusade in Asia* (Cambridge University Press, 2005) p. 1.

players. Counting his radio projects and newsreels, Luce built the first true multimedia corporation.[41]

In his February 1941 essay, which was published in *Life*, Luce gave popular expression to America's new role.[42] It laid the foundation for what eventually came to fruition as America's ascendancy rose. Luce wrote that while America was not in the conflict-at least not yet- the nation was faced "with great decisions." He acknowledged Amercia's almost endless wealth. "We know how lucky we are compared to all the rest of mankind. At least two-thirds of us are just plain rich compared to all the rest of the human family—rich in food, rich in clothes, rich in entertainment and amusement, rich in leisure, rich?"

Luce was born in China to missionary parents. His zeal to make American values those of the world is evident. He observed that "America was fast becoming the sanctuary of the ideals of civilization. For the moment it may be enough to be the sanctuary of these ideals. But not for long." What Luce had in mind next would become much of the philosophy behind American Empire. "It now becomes our time to be the powerhouse from which the ideals spread throughout the world and do their mysterious work of lifting the life of mankind from the level of the beasts to what the Psalmist called a little lower than the angels." Luce spoke for himself and other influential elites when he wrote, "It is only America as the dynamic center of ever-widening spheres of enterprise, America as the training center of the skillful servants of mankind, America as the Good Samaritan, really believing again that it is more blessed to give than to receive, and America as the powerhouse of the ideals of Freedom and Justice—out of these elements surely can be fashioned a vision of the Twentieth Century to which we can and will devote ourselves in joy and gladness and vigor and enthusiasm." This missionary's call from Luce rippled across the country over the next years. Public opinion increasingly became shaped by Luce's notion of "The American Century." The great question for America—and the world—was what America would do next.

It was kind to Luce's boyish joy that America did do something unique in the course of human events as the end of the war came into sight. Instead of going back to the antiquities-old playbook of subjecting newly vulnerable peoples to vengeful punishments, the Americans truly shocked the world. Starting at the Bretton Woods Conference in July 1944, the United States reached out to its weakened allies and, later, its vanquished enemies to make an unbelievable offer: We will give you the needed capital to start rebuilding your countries while the USA will carry the burden of protecting you from the aggressions of those who threaten you. In exchange, the United States asks for your support in expanding American-style capitalism around the world.

---

[41] Ibid.

[42] Henry Luce "The American Century" *Life*, February 17, 1941 http://www.informationclearinghouse.info/article6139.htm. Accessed January 22, 2018.

Further, to sweeten the deal—if it wasn't already sweet enough—the Americans declared that under the banner of free trade, foreign products and companies would have almost unrestricted access to the massive US market. Since the end of the American Civil War, the US market had been far and away the biggest single prize for all sorts of businesses. The unparalleled combination of a secure continental island; almost unlimited natural resources, including oil; a dynamic system of capital creation and allocation; a culture of entrepreneurship; and, government policy that overwhelmingly encourages and supports capitalism made the United States unique in human history. These forces have blended in such a way that providence appears to be behind it all.[43] For each of the past 15 decades, despite recessions, depressions, crashes, and bubbles, the US economy was richer at the end of the decade than it was at the beginning. In fact, the rise of the United States as the dominant global economic force has been *the* business story for the past 150 years. As John Steele Gordon observed, the United States became over a century ago—and remains today—"An Empire of Wealth." Equally important, the movement of those goods across the world's oceans would be secured—and paid for—by the US Navy and the American taxpayer.

When the Americans laid out this deal, no one could believe their ears. Here was the most dominant nation in history saying that its strategic vision for the future was a world built on consumers and producers. And, incredibly, nearly all the costs and burdens of securing that vision would be borne not by the losers. Rather, the winners of the war would do the heavy lifting for years to come. It all seemed good to be true. Yet, it was true.[44]

Without having to contend with Soviet aggression or worry about centuries-long rivalries with their neighbors, countries like the United Kingdom, France, West Germany, Japan, Taiwan, South Korea, and, later, India, Singapore, Thailand, China, and Vietnam could focus exclusively on rebuilding their economies. The security blanket provided by the United States ensured that business could be done without interference from others seeking to intrude on their growth.

The stimulus provided by American capital through programs like the Marshall Plan jump-started much of Western Europe and Eastern Asia. Later, the World Bank and International Monetary Fund would pick up the mantle and support economic growth around the globe. A significant portion of their prosperity would come from exporting to the United States. The eventual integration of China into the global economy initiated by President Nixon in 1972, and the collapse of the Soviet Union in 1990, assured for the foreseeable future that the dominant global idea would be capitalism as practiced in America.

Much of the world we live in today is, to a large part, the result of conscious decisions undertaken by American political leaders at the end of World War II and beyond. The US basket of guarantees is one of the most effective and longest-held

---

[43] Andrew R. Thomas & Timothy J. Wilkinson *The Customer Trap: How to Avoid the Biggest Mistake in Business* (Apress; 2015) p. 56.

[44] Ibid. p. 67.

promises in history. The results of America's gambit are clear: Over the past 74 years, more people have lived safer, richer, and healthier lives than ever before. Wars between major powers are a distant memory. Extreme poverty—the scourge of human experience—has been reduced by more than 70% and is still falling! Because of the American stabilization of the world since the end of World War II and the US' continued commitment to it, the United Nations has now realistically set a goal to eliminate ALL extreme poverty on the planet by 2030.[45] This achievement was not accomplished through increases in foreign aid. Instead, it was global economic growth underpinned by the American guarantees at Bretton Woods that made it happen.

After the War, nations who in "normal times" would have needed to spend tremendous sums to rebuild their armies and navies instead were able to invest in improving the lot of their populations: schools, electricity, sanitation systems, and innovation. The American military assured the peace. The American taxpayer paid the bill. Foreign companies and workers benefited immensely as well. The US Navy secured the world's shipping lanes. American taxpayers picked-up that check, too. Products moved seamlessly around the world, unlike any time in the past. Nations and businesses built the "American cost savings" into their forecast models. Traditional expenditures on national defense and supply chain security—historically huge costs only digestible to the richest countries and firms—became minor line items for everyone.

It seems, however, far too many Americans do not know what so much of the rest of the world does: the United States has been, and remains, the fulcrum of power on this planet. In a Pew Research Center survey conducted in April 2016, among US adults, only 54% identified the United States as the world's leading economic power, with China a distant second at 34%. Incredibly, this was the first time, in surveys dating back to 2008, that more than half of the American public named the United States as the leading economic power.[46]

It is disheartening to have to explain to so many Americans that its nation is indeed an Empire more, than Athens, Rome, or England ever were. This lack of knowledge might stem from the fact that most Americans are not comfortable with Empire. It goes against the grain of our own Revolution. Moreover, Empire has never been the stated goal of the United States. But that doesn't change the fact. History doesn't care.

---

[45] In 1990, the United Nations created several targets under the name of Millienium Goals. Target 1.A was to "halve, between 1990 and 2015, the proportion of people whose income is less than $1.25 a day". In 1990, nearly half of the population in the developing regions lived on less than $1.25 a day. This rate dropped to 14 per cent in 2015. Given the incredible progress made in this area, the UN has set 2030 as the year when all extreme povery can be eliminated. http://www.un.org/millenniumgoals/poverty.shtml, Accessed January 16, 2018.

[46] Pew Research Center "Public Uncertain, Divided Over America's Place in the World" May 5, 2016, http://www.people-press.org/2016/05/05/public-uncertain-divided-over-americas-place-in-the-world/. Accessed January 5, 2018.

The Unfolding Shape of American Empire

The American system of empire is much more a commercial one than others of the past. The establishment and growth of global capitalism is at its core. The resources of the US government and business are harnessed to that end. It benefits America and Americans to some extent. Yet, it benefits the greater world far more. In this unique American aspect, actors as diverse as the Pentagon, CIA, the US Treasury, Federal Reserve, Commerce Department, along with Wall Street bankers, manufacturers, transport firms, and retailers, tend to coalesce around sharing American economic practices abroad, and, more generally, promoting free capital movement and open trade.

Governments everywhere play a key role in underpinning capitalism, such as maintaining property rights, overseeing contracts, resolving disputes, taxation, maintaining currencies, etc. It is the American government, however, that has played an exceptional role in the creation of a fully global capitalist system. It is the immense strength of US capitalism that made globalization possible. What continues to make the American government distinctive is its vital role in managing and superintending capitalism on a worldwide plane.[47]

The containment of Communism, whether in the Cold War in Europe or the very hot wars in East Asia, was largely about ensuring that as many of the world's states as possible would be open to the accumulation of capital. Moreover, America's assurances that oil flows from the Middle East and other energy-rich parts of the world are available to fuel international trade and the global economy remain core to its Bretton Woods' guarantees.[48]

America's preeminence during and after the war was only further enhanced in the following decades. The USA enjoyed a postwar boom that was underpinned by relatively stable energy prices and significant domestic supply. This security of energy underpinned newly built US interstate highways and automated manufacturing, which allowed American companies to take full advantage of the consumer-driven economy. Further, the USA enjoyed unique advantages over the rest of the world in the postwar 1940s and 1950s. World War II had destroyed Europe's and Japan's infrastructure and dramatically weakened their ability to compete. US manufacturers benefited from enormous economies of scale relative to a divided Europe and a technologically underdeveloped Japan. Only their ability to find and exploit untapped opportunities limited the growth of American corporations.[49]

---

[47] Sam Gindin and Leo Panitch *The Making of Global Capitalism: The Political Economy Of American Empire* (Verso Books, 2012), p. 16.

[48] Ibid., p. 14.

[49] Edward Conard *Unintended Consequences: Why Everything You've Been Told About the Economy Is Wrong* (Penguin, 2012) p. 14.

A Quick Detour: The Rise of Natural Gas: A Mid-Twentieth Century Phenomena

Oil was the catalyst for the energy transition that marks the Carbon Age. A relative newcomer that continues to add weight to the dominance of modern hydrocarbon energy is natural gas. We haven't spoken a lot about it until now because natural gas really only became a critical component of modern society in the last 70 years. The invention of the Bunsen burner in 1885 (remember that item from high school chemistry?) finally allowed the controlled burning of natural gas, by mixing it with air in the right proportions, thus opening up new opportunities for the use of natural gas as a source of heat in applications such as cooking and heating. Still, transporting natural gas from wells to consumers was a difficult and dangerous challenge that took decades to overcome.

One of the first substantial natural gas pipelines was constructed in the USA in 1891, running for around 120 miles between gas wells in central Indiana to the city of Chicago. More significant pipeline construction began in the 1920s, and, after World War II, new welding techniques, along with advances in pipe rolling and metallurgy, further improved natural gas pipeline safety and reliability. The postwar boom lasted well into the 1960s, and allowed for the construction of hundreds of thousands of miles of pipeline around the world.[50] With safe and reliable transportation now assured, natural gas quickly became a widely distributed energy source; and new uses were soon discovered. These applications included using natural gas to heat homes and operate appliances, as well as the generation of electricity. Industries also began to use natural gas in manufacturing and processing plants. Natural gas is widely consumed in the pulp and paper, metals, chemicals, petroleum refining, stone, clay and glass, plastic, pharmaceutical, clothing, and food processing industries. We'll get back to the critical importance of natural gas in the present world shortly.

Global Capitalism and the Energy Shocks

By the late 1950s, Europe, Japan, and, later, other nations started getting their footing back. Global capitalism began to take hold, all the while supported by America's commitment to Bretton Woods and the uninterrupted flow of energy. The continued rise of the American economy, along with the surge in productivity from Europe, Japan, Southeast Asia, and parts of Latin America, began to put increasing strain on existing global energy supplies. While the USA remained the world's largest energy consumer and producer (both of oil and natural gas), demand at home and abroad

---

[50] Robin Wylie "A Brief History of Natural Gas" *Eni.com* https://www.eniday.com/en/education_en/history-natural-gas/. Accessed January 17, 2018.

was taxing domestic supply. Rumors about growing dependency on foreign energy sources to sustain US needs and those of her allies were getting louder.

By 1960, five oil-rich countries formed an alliance to regulate the supply and price of oil. These countries realized they possessed a nonrenewable resource. If they competed with each other, the price of oil would be so low that they would run out sooner than if oil prices were higher. OPEC (Organization of Petroleum Exporting Countries) held its first meeting in Baghdad. The five founding members were Iran, Iraq, Kuwait, Saudi Arabia, and Venezuela. OPEC registered with the United Nations on November 6, 1962. By the end of the decade, as global energy demand continued to surge, many wondered what the future would hold.

In 1973, the Organization of Arab Petroleum Exporting Countries (OAPEC)—a subgroup of OPEC—led by Saudi Arabia decided to halt sales to the United States for its support of Israel in the Yom Kippur war against Egypt, Syria, and other Arab nations. On October 19, immediately following President Nixon's request for Congress to make available $2.2 billion in emergency aid to Israel, OAPEC instituted an oil embargo on the United States. The embargo ceased US oil imports from participating OAPEC nations, and began a series of production cuts that altered the world price of oil. These cuts nearly quadrupled the price of oil from $2.90 a barrel before the embargo to $11.65 a barrel in January 1974.[51]

The shockwaves from this sudden rise in oil prices driven by a geopolitical event altered many aspects of the global economy. This spike in oil prices helped send most of the world's developed economies into a recession, staring in the USA. Massive wealth transfers from importing nations (primarily in the developed world) to the oil exporters were glaring. The combined petroleum earnings of oil exporters rose from $23 billion in 1972, before the embargo, to $140 billion by 1977.[52]

For the importers, in addition to the quadrupling of oil prices and the shortages that came with them, high levels of inflation were unleashed on their economies. By the end of 1977, the annualized inflation rate in the USA was over 6%. President Jimmy Carter in a televised speech compared the energy crisis of 1977 to "the moral equivalent of war." Inflation in 1978 rose another 9%. And, by December 1979, inflation topped 13%.[53]

For "Hydrocarbon Man"—as Daniel Yergin calls him—and the industrialized nations where he resided, the 1970s were marked by "rancor, tension, unease and gritty pessimism."[54] Of course, during that period, no one knew what lay ahead. Many wondered if chronically high inflation and rising energy prices would become the "new normal" for America going forward. Further, people were nervous that geopolitics was now a key determinant in the price of energy. And, most scary of all,

---

[51] Merrill, Karen. *The Oil Crisis of 1973-1974: A Brief History with Documents*. Boston: Bedford/St. Martin's, 2007, p. 17.

[52] Yergin, Daniel. *The Prize: the Epic Quest for Oil, Money, & Power*. New York: Free Press, 2009, p. 616.

[53] Inlation.EU http://www.inflation.eu/inflation-rates/united-states/historic-inflation/cpi-inflation-united-states-1978.aspx accessed December 13, 2017.

[54] Yergin, p. 635.

people questioned would oil-producing nations be able to gain greater influence over our lives? Each of these seemed distinctly possible—and events over the next several years would seem to confirm the worst of these fears.

In 1979, the Iranian revolution and Iran's subsequent war with neighboring Iraq led to a tripling of oil prices. Again the result was a recession in the USA and other advanced economies. In 1990, Iraq invaded Kuwait and threatened the Saudi oil-fields. The US and allied military buildup known as Desert Shield and, the eventual liberation of Kuwait known as Desert Storm, was marked by another tripling of global oil prices. Recession followed.

Between 2005 and 2008, rising oil demand from China and other emerging nations had many concerned about peak supply: meaning, apprehension that the amount of available oil would not be able to meet global demand. At the same time, continued tensions in the Middle East melded with the worries over peak supply. Speculators, sensing a market opportunity, leveraged their bets and, by July 2008, oil had risen to $145 per barrel: the highest level ever recorded.[55] Two months later, the investment bank Lehman Brothers collapsed on Wall Street and, the financial crisis, which led to The Great Recession, was underway. By 2009, as companies in American shed millions of jobs and consumers, many facing plunging home values and often foreclosures, stopped shopping, economic activity in the USA plummeted. Europe's economies were hit later by The Great Recession than that of the USA and took a big hit as the Euro crisis spread. Later, in 2010, China, Latin America, and the Middle East, whose economies had withstood the first rounds of the global slowdown, finally felt the effects. Energy use tumbled precipitously around the world, and prices along with them. As the world finally began to emerge from the hangover of the global financial crisis, economic activity began to pick up, as did the consumption and pricing of oil.

Over the years since the first energy "shock" in 1973, Americans became increasingly concerned that their national prowess—and future—was being held hostage to outside forces that could shape and manipulate energy prices: ultimately to the country's detriment. The popular view held that the American way of life was progressively being molded not so much by Americans themselves anymore. Instead, international oil companies, Middle Eastern sheikdoms, and powerful global cartels held greater influence over the lives of each American. There was certainly an element of truth here. Each economic downturn in the United States, and, consequently, around the world, since 1973, was fuelled by a spike in oil prices. Americans worried and wondered: *would this continue to be our future?* Like the "Death Star" in the *Star Wars* saga, was there a glaring vulnerability built into the American Empire that, if it was attacked, could bring it all crashing down? It sure seemed that way when George W. Bush and Barack Obama gave their State of the Union Addresses in 2006 and 2009, citing America's soft underbelly and the county's growing dependence on foreign energy imports.

---

[55] FedPrimeRate.com tracks the monthy price of West Texas Intermediate (WTI) crude from 2006 to the present. http://www.fedprimerate.com/crude-oil-price-history.htm. Accessed December 13, 2017.

Yet, just when it seemed all might be lost one day - and that the American Empire would succumb to the power of others manipulating the strings of energy -something happened that changed everything. As is so often the case, American ingenuity unpredictably entered into the picture.

America's Shale Energy Revolution

Ask an average group of people when the smartphone revolution began and you'll likely get some guesses that it was somewhere around the late 1990s. References to Blackberry's and Palm Pilots would populate the responses: and they'd be partly right.[56] I still miss my Blackberry, as the "press keys" remain much better suited to my fat fingers than touch screens... Work on integrating a mobile telephone with a computer and the Internet had started earlier in that decade and accelerated as the Web became more mainstream. Apple's introduction of the first iPhone in 2007 changed forever the world that would follow. The ease of use—particularly for people with skinny fingers—coupled with the style and look of the iPhone—redrew the boundaries and expanded the possibilities for what was possible when it came to personal communication.

While the iPhone debuted in 2007, the technologies that the smartphone integrated were nothing close to new. The telephone was invented in the Mid-Nineteenth Century. The first cellular call was made in 1973. Cellular phones gained widespread popularity by the early 1990s. Computers appeared in the first half of the Twentieth Century. As microprocessing dramatically improved, personal computers were introduced and mass-marketed in the 1980s. The telegraph—a Nineteenth Century invention—was the first fully digital communication system. In the 1960s, the US Defense Department contracted to build the ARPANET (Advanced Research Projects Agency Network), which laid the foundation for the Internet. The first message on ARPANET was sent in 1969. By the 1980s, the World Wide Web was under construction. And, by the 1990s, popular usage of the Internet went global. The smartphone integrated all of these older technologies into an easier, more accessible, more efficient, and more affordable platform. And, it changed the world.

The integration of old technologies into a new, revolutionary platform can also be observed through the development of America's shale energy resources. In this case, two old processes—drilling and "fracking"—have undergone significant upgrades in recent years. Interestingly, the current mix of horizontal drilling and hydraulic fracturing, and the smartphone, are about the same age. And, like the telephone, computer, and Internet, the technologies used in present-day shale energy extraction have been around a long time.

Human beings were making holes in the ground to gain access to water and salt for thousands of years. Many believe it was first the Chinese in 252 BC who

---

[56] For a good history of the development of the smartphone see Elizabeth Woyke's *The Smartphone: Anatomy of an Industry.* (New Press, 2014)

developed drilling techniques to access salt brine. The first wells were effectively large pits that gradually got narrower as they descended to about 300 feet. As the Chinese experimented, they later were able to drill narrower and deeper shafts. Sometimes flames or an explosion would rise up from the hole and kill people on the surface. This unknown, invisible, and deadly force was initially thought to be an evil spirit from the underworld. By 100 AD, however, the Chinese had learned that the invisible substance was not en evil spirit. Instead, if harnessed properly, it could be a tremendous source of heat. They identified the holes where the invisible substance came out of the ground, lit the holes, and placed the pots nearby. They could cook with it. This was the first known use of natural gas in history.[57]

Drilling into the Earth for water and salt continued to improve over centuries. In 1126 AD, the first "artesian" well with positive pressure (a flowing water well) was drilled by a group of monks in the French province of Artois.[58] In the early seventeenth century, the "Grenelle Well"—another French artesian water—implemented a dry rotary auger method and reached 1771 feet. It took 8 years.[59] Francis Drake's well in 1859 in Titusville, Pennsylvania was the first successful commercial venture designed to locate and extract oil. Using cable-assisted tooling, it drilled to 69 feet in about a week.

As oil demand grew, principally as the energy source for lighting, the next few years saw some radical experimentation in drilling and extraction methods. The use of "Roberts' Torpedoes" became a most popular method. Named after their inventor, Colonel E.A.L. Roberts, a veteran of both the Mexican War and Civil War, the first "torpedoes," which were encased in iron, contained somewhere between 15 and 20 pounds of gun powder. They were then lowered into the well, near to where it was believed the greatest amount of "fracture" of rock would occur once the torpedo was detonated. In November 1866, Roberts was awarded US Patent No. 59,936 for torpedoes. Later versions preferred nitroglycerin to gun powder. The process was as simple as it was successful. Filling the borehole with water provided Roberts his "fluid tamping" to concentrate concussion and more efficiently fracture surrounding oil strata. The technique had an immediate impact—production from some wells increased 1200 percent within a week of being "shot"—and the Roberts Petroleum Torpedo Company flourished.[60]

Needless to say, Roberts' notion of "fracturing" the subsurface rock to release any trapped organic material was a major breakthrough in the long history of human beings making holes in the Earth and extracting resources from them. Still, this was very dangerous business. As noted by John J. McLaurin in 1896, "A flame or a spark would not explode Nitro-Glycerin readily, but the chap who struck it a hard rap

[57] Mark Kurlansky *Salt: A World History* (Knopf Canada, 2011), p. 8.

[58] Elias Howard Sellards *Occurrence and Use of Artesian and Other Underground Water Issue 89 of Bulletin* (University of Florida Agricultural Experiment Station, 1907), p. 107.

[59] Pierre Hyacinthe Azaïs *Explanation and History of the Artesian Well of Grenelle* (University of Chicago, 1845), p. 9.

[60] David A. Waples *The Natural Gas Industry in Appalachia: A History from the First Discovery to the Tapping of the Marcellus Shale, 2nd ed.* (McFarland, 2012), p. 124.

might as well avoid trouble among his heirs by having had his will written and a cigar-box ordered to hold such fragments as his weeping relatives could pick from the surrounding district."[61] While nitroglycerin remained in use far into the Twentieth Century, other safer, and more effective, means were being sought to force trapped carbon to the surface.

At this point, it's important to take a step back and recognize that "fracturing"— or "fracking" as it has been popularly labeled in recent years—is a process done for the purpose of getting a specific kind of rock to give up its contents. Fracturing the rock is simply a means to an end. And, human beings have been doing it for more than a century and a half.

As we learned in high-school science class, there are three main types of rocks: sedimentary, metamorphic, and igneous. About 95% of the Earth's crust is made up of either igneous or metamorphic rocks. Only 5% of the Earth's crust contains sedimentary rock. Moreover, there are only three particular types of sedimentary rocks that can potentially contain usable oil and natural gas. They are shale, sandstone, and limestone. Within each kind of these sedimentary rocks rests the remains of long-dead, carbon-based organisms that fused with grains and mineral particles (also known as sediments) as water ran over them. Because these kinds of rocks are bound together by such small components, they are porous in nature, which means they are full of spaces that energy-rich carbon compounds can settle, later to be liberated in the form of either oil or gas.[62]

Shale is a sedimentary rock frequently mentioned as a natural fuel source. This is because of its abundance: More than 40% of all sedimentary rock is shale in its composition. Shale is produced when layers of carbon-rich mud are compressed until they harden into rock that retains those layers. One type of shale contains so much kerogen, the organic solid that gets processed into oil and gas, that it is called "oil shale."

Other types of especially porous rocks often form above shale beds, trapping the low-density carbon compounds that may rise through the mud that becomes shale in their spaces. Sandstone is one such rock, created from grains of minerals like quartz bound by other compounds, such as silica. Within sandstone beds such as Alberta, Canada's "tar sands," carbon compounds generally exist in liquid form, as crude oil, that in some cases also releases natural gas when brought to Earth's surface.

Like sandstone, carbonates are sedimentary rocks commonly found in conjunction with shale. Carbonates, however, are formed largely from remains of marine life, particularly shells and bones, combined with other minerals. Because of this, they are full of calcium and other compounds that lead to their classification: limestones, which contain calcium carbonate, and dolomites, which contain calcium magnesium carbonate.[63] The spaces between their fused fragments are where oil and gas may be found.

---

[61] John James McLaurin *Sketches in Crude Oil: Some Accidents and Incidents of the Petroleum Development in All Parts of the Globe* (Publisher: Author, 1896), p. 334.

[62] Darlene R. Stille *Sedimentary Rocks: A Record of Earth's History Exploring* (Capstone, 2008) p. 4.

[63] Ibid., p. 17.

To put this all another way, oil and natural gas together make petroleum. Petroleum, which is Latin for *rock oil*, is a fossil fuel, meaning it was made naturally from decaying plant and animal remains. It is a mixture of hundreds of different hydrocarbon molecules containing hydrogen and carbon that exist sometimes as a liquid (crude oil) and sometimes as a vapor (natural gas).

Over hundreds of millions of years, oil and natural gas were formed from the remains of prehistoric plants and animals—that's why they're called fossil fuels. These prehistoric plant and animal remains settled into the seas along with sand, silt, and rocks. As the rocks and silt settled, layer upon layer piled up in rivers, along coastlines, and on the sea bottom trapping the organic material. Without air, the organic layers could not rot away. Over time, increasing pressure and temperature changed the mud, sand, and silt into rock (known as source rock) and slowly "cooked" the organic matter into petroleum. Petroleum is held inside the rock formation, similar to how a sponge holds water.[64]

The oil and gas that formed in the source rock deep within the Earth moved upward through tiny connected pore spaces in the rocks. Some seeped out at the Earth's surface. Nonporous rocks or other barriers trapped most of the petroleum hydrocarbons. These underground traps of oil and gas are called reservoirs. Contrary to popular misconception, reservoirs are not underground "lakes" of oil; they are made up of porous and permeable rocks that can hold significant amounts of oil and gas within their pore spaces. Some reservoirs are hundreds of feet below the surface, while others are thousands of feet underground.

"Fracking" is the process used to break up, or "fracture", the porous, underground sedimentary rock formations that contain oil and natural gas. Once the source rock is fractured, its contents will migrate to the surface. Over time, human experimentation and tinkering began to move away from the nitroglycerin-based torpedoes of the nineteenth century toward safer and more sustainable fracking methods. On March 17, 1949, a team of petroleum production engineers performed the first commercial application of hydraulic fracturing about 12 miles east of Duncan, Oklahoma. Later that same day, personnel of Halliburton and Stanolind successfully fractured another oil well near Holliday, Texas using pressurized water as the catalyst. Hydraulic fracturing is a technique in which rock is fractured by a pressurized liquid. The process involves the high-pressure injection of "fracking fluid" (a kind of gel that is a mix of primarily water, sand, and other proppants suspended with the aid of thickening agents) into a well bore to create cracks in the deep-rock formations through which natural gas, petroleum, and brine would flow more freely. When the hydraulic pressure is removed from the well, small grains of hydraulic fracturing proppants (either sand or aluminum oxide) hold the fractures open.[65] The technique was developed and patented by Stanolind (later known as Pan American Oil Company) and exclusively license issued to Halliburton. By 1953, all credentialed oil and gas service companies were given access to this new process.

---

[64] Energy4me.org "Petroleum and Natural Gas" http://energy4me.org/all-about-energy/what-is-energy/energy-sources/petroleum/. Accessed January 2, 1018.

[65] American Oil & Gas Historical Society, "Shooters" – a fracking history", https://aoghs.org/technology/hydraulic-fracturing/. Accessed, January 6, 2018.

Tinkering and experimentation continued as more than one million wells were drilled using this gel-based hydraulic fracturing method.[66]

Still, there were limitations to how much this process could achieve. People within the energy industry knew there was more, probably a lot more, petroleum trapped within sedimentary rock, particularly shale that the current cocktail couldn't access. The questions were how to get it? And, just as important, how to do it as inexpensively as possible?

In a classic case of American-style creativity, risk-taking, and entrepreneurialism, Nick Steinsberger, a 34-year old petroleum engineer working for Mitchell Energy, unleashed one of the biggest "open sesames" of the modern era on June 11, 1998. On that day, Steinsberger added massive amounts of injected water to the cocktail, which cracked the shale beneath S.H. Griffin Well #4 in North Texas. A few days later, to the astonishment of everyone, the well was producing more natural gas than could ever be imagined. Steinsberger had figured out how to force shale to give up all of its hidden treasure.[67] Nevertheless, Steinsberger's breakthrough wasn't enough to make America's shale energy revolution a reality. To make it possible, significant advances in drilling techniques needed to occur as well.

Horizontal drilling is the process of drilling a well vertically from the surface to a subsurface location just above the target oil or natural gas reservoir (commonly called the "kickoff point"). This process is similar to the drilling process for a traditional vertical oil or gas well. The difference is that a horizontal well deviates or turns the well bore horizontally to intersect the oil and natural gas reservoir at a specific entry point.

The end result is a better pathway for oil and natural gas is created to reach the well bore. In a very basic sense, a horizontal lateral is like a drainage ditch a farmer might use to drain water from their fields; horizontal drilling has two key benefits. First, the flow of oil and natural gas into the well bore is dramatically increased. In a traditional vertical well, approximately 50 feet of the well bore is open to capture oil and natural gas. A horizontal lateral can go a mile or farther into the reservoir rock formation, exposing more oil and natural gas reserves to the well bore. Additionally, and this is the big point here, horizontal drilling has led to reducing the overall footprint of oil and natural gas activity. As the example in the following graphic shows, this horizontal well produces the energy of 32 oil or natural gas wells. Prior to horizontal drilling technology, you would have had to drill 32 wells in the area to get the same energy production as 1 horizontal well.[68] The economies of scale that horizontal drilling represent are stunning.

---

[66] Ibid.

[67] Russell Gold *The Boom: How Fracking Ignited the American Energy Revolution and Changed the World* (Simon and Schuster, 2015), p. 115–117.

[68] Ohio Oil and Gas Assocition "Ohio Shale Plays" http://www.ooga.org/?page=OhioShalePlays. Accessed January 19, 2018.

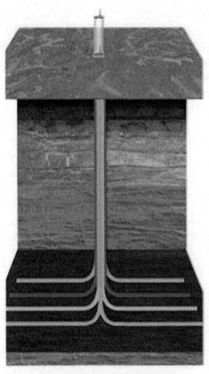

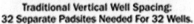

Traditional Vertical Well Spacing: Idealized Horizontal Well Spacing:
32 Separate Padsites Needed For 32 Wells.   1 Padsite Yields Up To 32 Wells.

Photo Courtesy of the Ohio Oil and Gas Association

When drilling into a hydrocarbon bearing formation 100 feet thick, vertical drilling would allow an operator to contact 100 feet of rock, which would reduce the potential recovery to whatever oil or gas might flow into that length of pipe. Horizontal drilling now allows these same operators to drill and set pipe for a mile or more horizontally through this same rock formation. The driller is now contacting and fracturing 5200 feet of rock rather than 100 feet, which exponentially multiplies expected well recovery rates and provides massive economies of scale.[69] The technology employed is so advanced and exacting that drillers today can hit a target at the end of a drill string that is 10,000 feet vertical with a mile-long horizontal section that is no more than a few inches in diameter.[70]

In the USA over the past 12 years, the precision and scale of hydraulic fracturing and horizontal drilling have combined with unique American characteristics to give

---

[69] David Blackmon "Horizontal Drilling: A Technological Marvel Ignored", *Forbes*, January 28, 2013   https://www.forbes.com/sites/davidblackmon/2013/01/28/horizontal-drilling-a-technological-marvel-ignored/#1aec4e326f11. Accessed January 6, 2018.

[70] Ibid.

the nation's shale energy revolution its full weight. Carbon-containing shale rock is located in many different regions around the world. It is not exclusively within the United States. The fracturing and drilling techniques now being used are widely known to anybody with an Internet connection. Still, the shale energy revolution remains almost an exclusively American affair. This is not to say that other nations are not exploring—or already exploiting—this natural resource. The UK, Argentina, Ukraine, and China, among others, are ramping up their domestic shale energy industries. Yet, it is in America where the results have been truly staggering. The reason for the tremendous success in the USA can be attributed to some particular moving parts that have coalesced around shale energy to make it all possible.

First, of course, is geology. In this respect, nature has been tremendously kind to the USA. The conditions needed to unfold over hundreds of millions of years to generate carbon-producing shale rock occurred in many places across America's geology. Luck seemingly has its privileges.

Next is the distinctive American way that property rights and mineral rights are viewed. In every other nation in the world, the owner or leaser does not hold any mineral rights attached to any piece of private property. Instead, the national government controls them. Any decision on how to access those minerals is a government decision at the highest levels. In the USA, the opposite is the case. Mineral rights are privately held and can be passed to the new property owner, or held separately. This has meant that those who own mineral rights are able to allow energy exploration companies to do their work.

Doing the work is no easy matter. America's long history of energy development throughout the Carbon Age has created generations of the world's top geologists, petroleum engineers, geophysicists, surveyors, pipeline layers, drillers, welders, and journeymen. The collective learning in these fields over decades has given America all the labor she's needed to make the shale energy revolution come to life.

Much of the requisite capital necessary to fund America's shale energy revolution (estimated by many to already be more than $1 trillion since 2007) emanates from the world's most sophisticated financial system. While the US financial system has taken a public beating in recent years—some of it well-deserved—there is nowhere in the world where the allocation of capital occurs with greater efficiency and speed. The ability for shale energy entrepreneurs to align with sources of capital is one of the least reported—and most important—stories on financial development over the last decade.

The energy infrastructure that was already in place in America prior to the shale energy revolution provided the backbone to its recent stunning growth. By the 1990s, there were nearly a million miles of gas and oil pipeline across the country. Refining and storage facilities were well developed. The new infrastructure that has been constructed since 2007 enhances an already well-developed energy system.

We can look back at the last decade or so with complete hindsight. Even now, it needs to be remembered that it was entrepreneurs, financiers, and risk takers, who, without the benefit of knowing where it would go, got onboard the shale energy train. They made so much of it possible. This very American style of bold—some might say reckless—entrepreneurship is so often desired by the rest of the world, yet rarely found outside America's borders.

Finally, at any turn over the past decade, the government could have stepped in and changed the pace or direction. At the national level, both the Bush and Obama Administrations maintained an arm's-length distance from what was unfolding. Driven by the greater need to secure more domestic energy supply, the Federal Government did nothing of consequence to stop the development of American shale energy. When confronted with challenges from opponents of fossil fuels and those concerned about their increasing use, both Presidents opted to use the federalism provision and outsource the final decision to the States themselves. As a result, America's shale energy revolution has been driven much more by what happens at the local and state level than in Washington. This devolution of political power is something that doesn't get enough attention by today's Beltway-obsessed culture. The experimentation that marks American entrepreneurialism is also manifested by the tinkering which takes place every day across America's 50 states and its thousands of local governments.

All of this—technological advance, luck, and unique societal attributes—have aligned to bring us to this point. Every day, American energy firms and entrepreneurs continue to explore ways to reduce inefficiencies, increase their profits, and consistently produce more energy. American investors—and, now increasingly, foreign ones—calculate and recalculate their returns on capital, seeking to maximize the best position possible. American political leaders and civil servants at all levels of government pursue solutions to best manage this change for their constituents. It is not hyperbole to say that we are living at an inflection point. We are at the beginning stages of a new ascendancy of American energy—and Empire. The United States has become once again the largest energy-producing nation on Earth. The implications derived from America's shale energy revolution are now beginning to reveal themselves.

Business and Geopolitical Implications of American Shale Energy

3

Chapter Highlights

- High-quality and low-cost domestic Natural Gas Liquids (NGLs) are fuelling a renaissance in US manufacturing.
- Appalachia is positioned to be the natural gas capital of America, and the center of advanced plastics production in the world.
- American exports of shale energy are surging, providing new opportunities for US firms and the economy.
- Driven by domestic political considerations and its new energy security, America's commitment to the post-World War II international system is waning.
- American foreign policy will be much more reactive, unpredictable, and insular than anytime in the past.
- With American security guarantees being removed from around the world, the threat of major wars and conflicts will reappear, as geopolitics "returns to history."

Couldn't This All Just Be Hype?

It wouldn't be a stretch to consider the earlier portion of this book as optimistic, even wildly so. The argument that America's shale energy revolution is relatively young and will continue to trend upward assumes several favorable conditions going forward. A major alteration in one or more of these conditions could put things in a whole different light:

- The current assumptions for long-term natural gas and oil supplies are accurate
- Capital flows to current and future shale energy plays will remain vigorous

© The Author(s), under exclusive licence to Springer International Publishing AG, part of Springer Nature 2018
A. R. Thomas, *American Shale Energy and the Global Economy,* SpringerBriefs in Business, https://doi.org/10.1007/978-3-319-89306-8_3

- Energy pricing levels remain profitable for operators and investors
- Demand stays relatively high for these sources of energy

President Obama observed in his 2012 State of the Union Address "We have a supply of natural gas that can last America nearly one hundred years." When the President of the United States says something like this in such a setting, it appears to be definitive. In reality, it is only an estimate. There could be less—potentially much less—than 100 years of supply in the ground. Of course, there could be more. No one really knows, and if they tell you they *do* know, they are only really guessing. Estimates of future reserves are at best marginal attempts to quantify how much energy would be recoverable using current technology and practices. What is rarely taken into account- because of the level of difficulty of seeing into the future- is what the final cost of extraction will be. As energy prices flucuate regularly, today's potential windfall can easily become tomorrow's loser. To date, energy companies have only tapped a tiny fraction of the known shale formations in the country, so data points on recoveries, gas quality, flow rates, and other metrics are few in number.[1]

In September 2017, a dozen large shareholders in US shale energy firms got together to discuss how they could get those companies to start making money. The dirty little secret is that shale energy in America has remained a lousy bet for most investors. Since 2007, shares in an index of US producers fell 12%, while the S&P 500 rose more than 80%. Further, energy companies spent nearly $300 billion more than they generated from operations on shale investments.[2] It seems each time investors start asking when they can expect a decent return on their investment, the energy companies "move the goalposts" and tell them regular profits are just around the corner.[3] This finds many investors getting skittish about their current investments, and reconsidering future infusions of capital. The lower oil prices that marked the period 2014 to mid-2017 tested the faith of the investment community in shale energy firms. A return to low prices could considerably reduce the amount of future capital available to the industry for expansion.

When America's shale energy revolution broke out, interest rates and the costs of capital were abnormally low—and remained so for many years. Government stimulus and subsequent central bank interest rate manipulation in the wake of the global financial crisis forced capital into more risky areas in pursuit of better returns: areas where investment may have not normally flowed. Had interest rates been appreciably higher in the period from 2008 to 2017, America's shale energy industry may not have received the incredible levels of investment that made the revolution possible in the first place. Going forward, a rise in the cost of capital—coupled with continued low returns on investment—could turn down the spigot of investors.

Regarding demand, there is a fundamental assumption that a surging global population- enjoined with expanding prosperity- will naturally require more and more

---

[1] Charles R. Morris *Comeback: America's New Economic Boom* (Public Affairs, 2013) p. 36.

[2] Bradley Olson and Lynn Cook "Wall Street Tells Frackers to Stop Tallying Barrels, Focus on Profits" *Wall Street Journal*, December 7, 2017, p. A1.

[3] Ibid. p. A10.

energy production. This assumption is what surely keeps many investors in for the long haul. But what if world population growth fails to be so dramatic; if an external event—disease, cataclysmic war, natural calamity, etc.—entered into the equation? Or, say, a political or economic shock crushes the tremendous gains of the recent decades and send billions back into poverty? Or, even if the global population continues to get bigger and richer, might the gains from energy efficiencies and new energy technologies reduce the need for more shale energy production?

Each of these is a legitimate question and deserves consideration when it comes to assessing the future of America's shale energy revolution. Such scenarios could eventually delay, halt, or even retard the progress that has been made so quickly. By 2018, America's shale energy revolution was merely 12 years old. Prior to its arrival on the scene, forecasts of a dark and dour future reigned. What if a worst-case scenario becomes a reality and America's shale energy revolution burns itself out in the next decade or two?

Nevertheless, to simply write off America's shale energy revolution as hype or just a blip on the radar would be dangerous. Even if it lasts only another 10 years, discounting what has already happened, and what is currently occurring, America's shale energy revolution has already inexorably shaped the American and global economy. As Charles Morris points out, "The golden age of American manufacturing is often placed between 1948-1968 - only twenty years. We shouldn't turn up our noses at another run like that."[4]

The "Streams" of Shale Energy

I have made every effort to avoid using industry lingo in this book. Each area of specialization has its own lexicon, acronyms, and ways of articulating things. The energy industry is no exception. Nevertheless, there are a few key terms that should be understood to help better contextualize what the business implications of American shale energy are. When you fill up your car with gasoline or pay your natural gas heating bill, you are the final step in a long chain of businesses that provide energy to you. The entire chain is known as the "Energy Industry," and it is divided into three major components: *upstream*, *midstream*, and *downstream*.

The *upstream* of the energy industry finds and produces crude oil and natural gas. The *upstream* is sometimes known as the exploration and production (E&P) sector. It is within the *upstream* where the tremendous advances in hydraulic fracturing and horizontal drilling occurred to make the shale energy revolution possible in the first place.

The *midstream* portion of the energy industry processes, stores, markets, and transports commodities such as crude oil, natural gas, and natural gas liquids. The *midstream* provides the vital link between where the exploration and production took place and the population centers where *downstream* customers are located.

---

[4] Morris *Comeback: America's New Economic Boom* (Public Affairs, 2013) p. 40.

The *downstream* is the last stage of the process, and involves the processing, selling, and distribution of natural gas and oil-based products. The *downstream* includes oil refineries, petrochemical plants, petroleum products distributors, retail outlets, and natural gas distribution companies. These *downstream* players sell their oil and natural gas by-products to manufacturers, who use the by-products to make hundreds of thousands of finished goods such as the gasoline to fill your tank, the natural gas to heat your home, tires, toothpaste, fertilizers, antifreeze, pesticides, toys, clothing, medicines, etc.[5]

Natural Gas Liquids (NGLs) and American Manufacturing

America's surging abundance in shale energy is altering the structure and relationships within the *streams* and beyond. I described earlier the transformation that has recently taken place in the production of agricultural chemicals. In less than a decade, America went from being the world's largest importer of fertilizers, pesticides, and herbicides to, once again, the largest producer and exporter. Developments in the *upstream* opened up new sources of shale energy that were previously unattainable. Investment in the infrastructure needed to move the new shale energy (the *midstream*) into the value chain surged, allowing the processing facilities (the *downstream*) to turn the oil and natural gas liquids into finished products. The growth in the *downstream* provided an opportunity for our client to sell their heat exchangers to the agricultural chemical processing plants that were coming online.

The expansion of all three *streams* driven by domestic shale energy growth is creating new business opportunities across America. As little as 12 years ago, grave concerns were being raised that the USA would not be able to meet her natural gas needs. Imports of natural gas liquids (NGLs) spiked, and it appeared America was going to add natural gas to its list of foreign addictions. In response, many US industries tied to petrochemicals headed out the door to produce overseas. Those who stayed behind significantly reduced their footprint.

Today, it's a completely different story. It starts with NGLs. During the exploration and production process, both oil and natural gas migrate to the surface. Petroleum and gas are then separated. At processing plants, natural gas can be broken down into liquids, the principal ones being ethane, butane, propane, heptanes, hexane, and pentanes. Each of these serves as the critical foundations for so many indispensible aspects of our lives.

Ethane is mainly used to produce ethylene, which is then used by the petrochemical industry to produce a range of intermediate products, most of which are converted into plastics. Ethane can also be used directly as a fuel for power generation, either on its own or blended with natural gas.

---

[5] Petroleum Services Association of Canada" Industry Overview" https://www.psac.ca/business/industry-overview/. Accessed January 24, 2018.

Butane has many applications, including as a liquid fuel, a propellant for aerosol sprays, and a base for the production of other petrochemicals. Although some normal butane is used as a fuel for lighters, most of it is blended into gasoline, especially during the cooler months.

Pentane is a natural gasoline (also known as pentanes plus) that can be blended into the fuels used in internal combustion engines, particularly motor gasoline. In the United States, natural gasoline is added to fuel ethanol as a denaturant to make the ethanol undrinkable, which is required by law. About half of US natural gasoline production is exported to Canada where it is used as a diluent to reduce viscosity of heavy crude oil, so that the crude oil can be more easily moved in pipelines and railcars.

Propane is used primarily as a heat source. Most of the propane consumed in the United States is used as a fuel, generally in areas where the supply of natural gas is limited or not available. This use is highly seasonal, with the largest consumption occurring in the fall and winter months. Propane sold as a fuel for the consumer market is generally defined as HD-5, which contains a minimum of 90% propane by volume, with small quantities of other hydrocarbon gases. HD-10, which contains up to 10% propylene, is the accepted standard for propane in California.

There are two general market categories for propane: consumer (primarily as fuel) and nonconsumer (primarily for nonfuel or feedstock uses). There are four major consumer uses of propane: in homes, for space heating and water heating; for cooking; for drying clothes; and for fueling gas fireplaces, barbecue grills, and backup electrical generators; on farms, for heating livestock housing and greenhouses, for drying crops, for pest and weed control, and for powering farm equipment and irrigation pumps; in businesses and industry, to power fork lifts, electric welders, and other equipment; and as a fuel for on-road internal combustion engine vehicles such as cars, school busses, or delivery vans, and non-road vehicles such as tractors and lawn mowers.[6]

The non-consumer market for propane is the petrochemical industry. The primary use of propane in the petrochemical industry is as a feedstock, along with ethane and naphtha, in petrochemical crackers to produce ethylene, propylene, and other olefins. Propylene and the other olefins may be converted into a variety of products, mostly plastics and resins, and also glues, solvents, and coatings.

Heptanes are widely used in the manufacturing of paints, sealants, and pharmaceuticals. While *hexane* can be found in chemicals that are used to make shoes, leather products, and roofing, these chemicals can also be used to extract cooking oils (such as canola oil or soy oil) from seeds; for cleansing and degreasing a variety of items; and in textile manufacturing.

---

[6]U.S. Department of Energy "Natural Gas Liquids Primer With a Focus on the Appalachian Region" December 2017, p. 2–4. https://www.energy.gov/sites/prod/files/2017/12/f46/NGL%20 Primer.pdf. Accessed January 24, 2017.

As America's shale energy revolution has taken root, companies that use these NGLs in their manufacturing processes have benefitted immensely. Next Generation Films is a Lexington, Ohio-based firm that makes specialty plastic packaging for the food industry. Next Generation Films has taken full advantage of its proximity to shale energy production and America's newfound growth in NGLs, particularly ethylene that comes from ethane. Since 2015, the firm has invested $20 million to expand its film plants, bag plant, conversion center, and warehouse in Lexington. Sales have increased by nearly 1/3 to over $400 million while hiring continues apace.[7]

US manufacturers like Next Generation Films are now regularly benefiting from an increased supply of low-cost, high-quality NGLs. This gives a large competitive advantage to US firms versus manufacturers in other countries that do not have an abundant supply of quality NGLs at their disposal. The American Fuel & Petrochemical Manufacturers association estimates that feedstocks account for 60–70% of the total cost to produce petrochemicals. Even a small drop in the cost of these feedstocks is a major benefit to US manufacturers. Since natural gas prices in the United States fell by 75% between 2005 and 2016, while remaining flat or rising in most of the rest of the world, US manufacturers that use domestic NGLs have enjoyed a significant competitive advantage.[8]

Quality is something that is taken for granted until it can't be found. The past practice of offshoring NGL and petrochemical production from the USA to lower-cost markets has often come at the expense of quality and product safety. Numerous incidents involving poor-quality NGLs made in China have blared across the headlines in recent years. Products from tainted pet food that killed and sickened thousands of animals, to toys that were covered in lead-based paint, to personal care products like toothpaste that were deemed poisonous, had US firms reevaluating their original decision to go to China in the first place. With America's shale energy revolution well underway, the USA is seeing many of the firms that once departed now returning, as high-quality domestic petrochemicals and NGLs have fallen in price. Reshoring, as it is known, is the relocation of manufacturing and operations back to the home market. It is not a surprise that one of the top reasons firms reshore, according to research from the Reshoring Initiative, is quality control.[9]

Bison Gear & Engineering Corp. is a St. Charles, Illinois-based manufacturer that has provided motor, gear reducer, gear motor, and complete system solutions to customers around the world since 1960. In the 1990s, the company followed many in its industry and sought greener pastures in lower-cost China. After a few years, it

---

[7] Plastics News "Next Generation Films Investing $20 million in Ohio Expansion" January 21, 2015, p. 16.

[8] Kinder Morgan Corp. "The Role of Natural Gas Liquids (NGLs) in the American Petrochemical Boom" White Paper https://www.kindermorgan.com/content/docs/White_Natural_Gas_Liquids.pdf. Accessed January 24, 2018.

[9] The Reshoring Initiative is a non-profit clearinghouse of research and case studies on U.S. firms that have reshored their operations. http://www.reshorenow.org/presentations/

became clear that reduced production costs in China came with a terrible price. Citing the resurgency of natural gas production in the USA and the ability to control the quality of its supply chain, Bison reshored its Chinese operations back to America in 2012. New jobs were added.[10]

It seems a sustainable formula for a renaissance in American manufacturing is taking hold, driven by the shale energy revolution. Abundant domestic natural gas is making cheaper, high-quality domestic NGLs more and more available to US petrochemical producers, manufacturers of finished goods, and consumers. Once again the world's single largest consumer market is poised for resurgence in its "Made in the USA" label. In 2008, Brooks Bros. bought a plant in Haverhill, Mass., and has moved nearly all of its suit production there, mostly from offshore locations, says John Martynec, who heads domestic manufacturing for the venerable designer and retailer. Employment at the plant has increased to 475 from 300. High-quality NGLs are crucial to ensuring the integrity of Brooks Bros.' design and manufacturing processes. "Making it" in the USA guarantees product quality and also bolsters Brooks Bros.' fast-growing international business. "A U.S. product is perceived as a luxury item in other areas of the world," he says.[11]

Shale Energy and Transformation in Appalachia

There is a living case study currently unfolding in Appalachia that further illustrates how the value chain of America's shale energy revolution is evolving in real time. In many ways, Appalachia has been the template for so much of what is right about the revolution. Natural gas from across Appalachia is arguably some of the richest as it relates to natural gas liquids.

The two shale rock formations that dominate the region are the *Marcellus* and the *Utica*. The *Marcellus* stretches across the Appalachian basin—from upstate New York south through Pennsylvania to West Virginia and west to parts of Ohio. It is named after the small town of Marcellus, New York. When the industry speaks of exploring and producing shale energy gas, it often refers to it as a "shale play." The Marcellus was one of the first shale plays to be tapped in America, after the Barnett Shale formation in Texas. The other "shale play" is the *Utica*, which is named after the city of Utica, New York. The Utica's shale lies under most of New York, Pennsylvania, Ohio, and West Virginia, and extends under adjacent parts of Ontario and Quebec in Canada and Kentucky, Maryland, Tennessee, and Virginia in the United States. In the *Marcellus*, energy is found in shale rock to depths of up to 9000 feet. The *Utica* is not as deep, normally found about 5000 feet below ground surface.

---

[10] Alejandra Cancino and Cheryl V. Jackson, "More manufacturing work returns to U.S. shores." *Chicago Tribune*. March 27, 2012, p. C1.

[11] Paul Davidson. "Some apparel manufacturing 'reshoring' to USA." *USAToday*. July 5, 2013. http://www.usatoday.com/story/. Accessed January 25, 2018. money/business/2013/07/04/some-apparel-manufacturing-returns-to-us/2454075/.

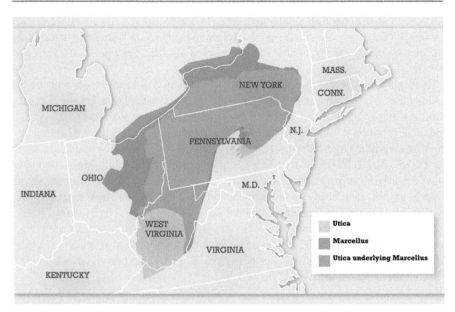

Image courtesy of Marcellus Shale Coalition

While shale rock in both the *Marcellus* and *Utica* contains hydrocarbons, what makes them geologically special is the kind of hydrocarbons they contain. Not all natural gas is the same. "Dry" natural gas is made up almost entirely of methane, and not much else. There is lots of value in "dry gas"—as it is known. After minimal processing, dry gas can be transported via pipelines to consumers around the country who need it for things like home heating and electrical generation. Because of the shale energy revolution, much cleaner "dry gas" is quickly replacing dirtier coal as America's largest source of electricity. While dry gas is a hydrocarbon and does emit CO_2 when burned, the emissions are far less than those caused by the burning of coal. According to the US Environmental Protection Agency, since the advent of America's shale energy revolution in 2006, spurred by the rising use of cleaner dry gas over coal since, the nation's overall carbon footprint has been reduced by more than 12%.[12] "Wet" natural gas, on the other hand, contains compounds like ethane and butane that we learned about previously. It is from "wet gas" where natural gas liquids (NGLs) originate.

The *Marcellus* and the *Utica* are rich in both dry and wet gas. This unique combination is making the *Marcellus* and *Utica* the natural gas centers of America and, quite possibly soon, the world. At present, the Appalachian basin currently supplies

---

[12] U.S. EPA, "Climate Change Indicators: U.S. Greenhouse Gas Emissions" August 2016 https://www.epa.gov/climate-indicators/climate-change-indicators-us-greenhouse-gas-emissions. Accessed January 27, 2018.

42% of all US natural gas demand. And, output is rising.[13] The region has been at the forefront of innovation when it comes to exploration and production. For example, lateral drilling there has reached over 20,000 feet—nearly four miles! Moreover, rather than the old formula of 1 drilling rig for 1 platform, advances have led to a typical platform containing up to 12 producing wells at once. And, experimentation in the cocktail used in the hydraulic fracturing process has led to long-term improvements in extraction rates. In just the last few years, rig operators in Appalachia have been able to increase the yield from a single well by more than 60%.[14]

Of course, it is one thing to extract the hydrocarbons from the shale rock: Activity that the Appalachian Basin is certainly good at—and getting much better. Vital infrastructure in the midstream is also needed to be able to move, store, and process the natural gas as it moves through the value chain. Until recently, there was a shortage of pipeline available to transport the natural gas from the wells. In addition, storage facilities were significantly lacking, which had the effect of reducing what producers could take out of the ground. If you can't store it, you lose it. So, better to keep in the ground in the first place until you are sure that it will move unhindered downstream. Finally there were no "cracker plants" in the area, which further complicated any development. A *"cracker"* is industry-speak lingo for a facility that takes wet gas and breaks it into smaller molecules, to create ethylene. The closest "crackers" were on the East Coast. Therefore, the time, effort, and cost required moving the wet gas to a cracker plant and to ship it back to the region for integration into manufacturing were highly inefficient.

The last 2 years have seen an incredible transformation in the downstream of shale energy in Appalachia. More than $30 billion of pipelines have been laid across the region allowing for natural gas to flow where it can be processed quickly and inexpensively. New storage facilities, which allow for the ability to manage inventory, are now underway. At the beginning of 2018, the US Department of Energy announced plans to loan a consortium of regional energy players up to $1.9 billion for the construction of storage facilities. Federal support through guaranteed financing of energy projects is nothing new. Tesla, the famed electric car company, got its start with a nearly half billion-dollar loan from the Department of Energy. Finally, construction is already underway in southwestern Pennsylvania for a $9 billion cracker plant that is being built by Shell, which will be operational by the early 2020s.

The investment behind all of this activity is driven by the continued low cost of natural gas liquids, principally ethylene, and the availability of shale energy in the region. This has led to a tremendous level of optimism for making the region the advanced plastics capital of the world. The "Shale Crescent"—as the region is now being branded—is uniquely positioned to be vertically integrated in every sense of the term. Ethylene is of particular interest because the region is already the world

---

[13] Liubov Georges "The World's Most Innovative Gas Field" Oilprice.com, Jan 20, 2018, https://oilprice.com/Energy/Energy-General/The-Worlds-Most-Innovative-Gas-Field.html.   Accessed January 27, 2018.

[14] Ibid.

leader in the research, development, and production of advanced plastics and polymers. In Ohio, it is the State's largest single industry, at around $32 billion annually in sales.[15] For decades, long-time global players such as Goodyear, Lubrizol, Omnova, Bridgestone, Eaton, Alcoa, and many others have collaborated with world-class researchers at the University of Akron, Case Western Reserve University, Carnegie Mellon University, West Virginia University, and the University of Pittsburgh to foster and commercialize the latest advances in rubber, advanced plastics, and polymers. The introduction of localized raw materials (ethylene) into this already existing ecosystem is creating critical mass. While advanced plastics is not nearly as sexy and glamorous as Silicon Valley's gadgets and gizmos, the potential economic impact of vertical integration within the Appalachian Basin is every much as formidable.

Similar to Silicon Valley, where trillions of dollars of government investment made it all possible, government is empowering private enterprise across the Appalachian Basin to nurture this burgeoning opportunity, all the while ensuring public safety and care for the environment. In Ohio, for example, all of the underground water in the State has been geo-mapped. Ohioans know precisely where their water is. No oil and gas well permits are issued for any activity within 500 feet of underground water. Rigorous standards and regular inspections assure that there has never been oil or gas well leakage into Ohio's water supply since the advent of modern shale energy production. Moreover, vertical injection wells have been banned in Ohio. Injection wells were used in the past to bury residue fracking fluid at depths of up to 20,000 feet, often drilling right through geologic plates. In many cases, the depth of the well would alter the delicate balance of the plates and trigger an earthquake. Pennsylvania and West Virginia have followed Ohio's lead and developed similar regulatory regimes. Interestingly, New York, which has not mapped its groundwater, has banned all activities around horizontal drilling and hydraulic fracturing.

This is not to say, however, that the Federal Government has outsourced the oversight of shale energy extraction and production exclusively to the States. To the contrary, the Feds have remained very involved in creating new regulations and enforcing existing ones around the public interest. As part of an Executive Order issued from the Trump Administration in December 2017, the Federal Energy Regulatory Commission (FERC) is working to establish consistency, predictability, and timeliness in the environmental review and permitting of pipeline and other major infrastructure projects and to complete all environmental reviews in a timely manner. The Pipeline and Hazardous Materials Safety Administration (PHMSA) is in the rule-making phase of the PIPES Act (Protecting Our Infrastructure of Pipelines and Enhancing Safety) that unanimously passed the Congress and was signed into law by President Obama on June 22, 2016. More rigorous pipeline inspection and the hiring and training of 10,000 new safety inspectors are core to the legislation. The US Environmental Agency continues to lead by assuring compliance; improving scientific understanding of hydraulic fracturing; providing

---

[15] Paul Boulier, "The Shale Value Chain" TEAMNEO, White Paper, June 23, 2015.

regulatory clarity and protections against known risks; ensuring the safe management of wastewater, storm water, and other by-products; and addressing air quality impacts associated with hydraulic fracturing activities.[16]

It's hard to put into words what the vertical integration occurring across Appalachia truly means. You really need to see it to believe it. The ability to do everything in one central location when it comes to advanced plastics, polymers, and rubber is remarkable. Further, the geographic location of the Appalachian Basin puts it within 500 miles of 60% of North America's population—and 70% of its total GDP. An expanding infrastructure is positioning the region for growing exports of the wet gas and NGLs, and other finished goods that will be produced locally. It has already meant jobs—tens of thousands of really good jobs for the local population—and huge sums of private capital into a region that has been traditionally challenged when it comes to attention for investors. Foreigners as well as Americans have already woken up to what's going on. A second cracker plant with an investment of $4 billion is in development in Eastern Ohio led by a consortium out of Thailand. It is safe to say that Appalachian shale gas production is here to stay and will dominate the national—and global—conversation about energy's future for years to come.[17]

The Rise of US Shale Energy Exports

The transformation of America as an increasingly dependent *importer* of energy to a growing *exporter* is one of the more recent developments of the shale energy revolution. The United States has been a net importer of energy since 1953. It still is today. Since 1953, America's surging economy demanded more energy than the nation could produce. As we saw earlier, while the USA continued to be a "global top-ten" producer of oil and natural gas, more and more imports were needed to make up the energy deficit. The strains and vulnerabilities of decreasing domestic energy security revealed themselves in the 1970s and remained potent until the arrival of the shale energy surge. Today, looking forward, it appears likely that the USA will once again return to the position of a net exporter of energy somewhere in the 2020s.[18] The implications of this are just beginning to emerge.

In November 2017, as President Trump was visiting China and speaking to that country's leaders, West Virginia and Alaska stood at the top of the agenda. In meetings with representatives from the China Energy Investment Corp. and Sinopec, the national oil company, an agreement was reached that will bring Chinese investment

[16] U.S. Environmental Protection Agency, "Unconventional Oil and Natural Gas Development" https://www.epa.gov/uog. Accessed January 28, 2018.

[17] Liubov Georges "The World's Most Innovative Gas Field" Oilprice.com, Jan 20, 2018, https://oilprice.com/Energy/Energy-General/The-Worlds-Most-Innovative-Gas-Field.html.   Accessed January 27, 2018.

[18] U.S. Energy Information Administration, "Annual Energy Outlook 2017", January 5, 2017 https://www.eia.gov/outlooks/aeo/pdf/0383(2017).pdf. Accessed January 28, 2018.

to West Virginia and Alaska in exchange for access to the shale gas produced from each state. With $83.7 billion in targeted capital, China will help to develop multiple projects in both states over a 20-year span. Projects will include power generation from natural gas, chemical manufacturing and storage of NGLs, and supplies of NGLs. In addition to the emerging multibillion-dollar natural gas deals with West Virginia and Alaska, China has already shown its desire to secure long-term access to oil produced from US shale energy. According to the US Energy Information Administration, China has already become one of the leading destinations for US light sweet crude oil.[19]

While foreign buyers and investors are targeting American NGLs and light sweet crude oil, the central focus of US shale energy exports is squarely on Liquefied Natural Gas (LNG). LNG is predominantly methane and used in heating and cooking as well as electricity generation and other industrial applications. For transport on the ocean, LNG is converted to liquid form for ease and safety of non-pressurized storage. LNG is shipped around the world in specially constructed massive seagoing vessels.

The global LNG market has changed exponentially in the past 20 years. As late as the early 2000s, the USA was constructing multibillion-dollar facilities along the Gulf Coast that would process LNG *imports*, looking to make up for America's energy deficit. Today, the opposite is the case. Massive capital investment is being plowed into LNG *export* infrastructure across the region: thanks to dramatic growth in US domestic natural gas production,

The export of LNGs from the USA has taken place in two waves. The first was typified by "Brownfield" conversion projects: taking preexisting *import* terminals and adding liquefaction capability and other necessary infrastructure improvements, so that they can *export* LNG. Existing US LNG import terminal owners/operators have added liquefaction/export capabilities as a means of adapting to the rapid growth in the global LNG market in the short term. However, as Kathleen Eisbrenner, the founder and CEO of NextDecade, an Houston-based LNG development company focused on export projects, points out, "there is only a finite number of existing LNG import terminals that can and will be converted to export facilities, and that number is not enough to satisfy future demand."[20]

According to Eisbrenner, the demand that made the first wave viable has continued to grow and that is leading to the second wave of US LNG exports. These are "Greenfield" projects, developed purposefully from the ground to meet the anticipated continued, growing, and new global LNG demand and prevent an impending global LNG supply shortage. New Greenfield projects "have a number of benefits,

---

[19] Luke Geiver "2017: The Year Shale Went Global" *North American Shale* December 18, 2017 http://northamericanshalemagazine.com/articles/2176/2017-the-year-shale-went-global. Accessed January 28, 2018.

[20] Matthew V. Veazey "Views from the Crest of LNG's Second Wave: NextDecade's Kathleen Eisbrenner" *Rigzone.com* November 01, 2017 https://www.rigzone.com/news/views_from_the_crest_of_lngs_second_wave_nextdecades_kathleen_eisbrenner-01-nov-2017-152299-article/ accessed Janaury 28, 2018.

including made-for-purpose design, and its associated cost and production efficiencies, as well as the ability for developers to select advantageous site locations with proximity and access to gas supply, among others."[21]

Of course, the USA is not the only place seeking to expand its LNG exports. Other nations such as Australia and Qatar are ramping up their LNG production as well, under the assumption that demand from importing nations will continue to rise. In 2018, China will overtake South Korea and Japan to become the world's largest LNG importer. Those three nations constitute about 60% of global LNG consumption. Much of the rise in demand from China comes from that nation's desire to reduce coal burning for household heating and replace it with much cleaner natural gas. In November 2017, at the Chinese Communist Party Congress, Premier Xi Jingping made a cleaner environment a top national priority. Chinese LNG imports rose almost 50% in 2017. If you've ever been to a Chinese city, the impact from all the coal burning reminds one why LNG is a far better option.

As LNG is a global commodity, its cost and availability ultimately determine the quality sold. For US newcomers, this will mean fierce competition from existing LNG exporters who have historically dominated this business. In addition, the increased complexity of doing cross-border trade; the challenges that arise from both physical and cultural distance; and the higher costs to the enterprise that global business requires will all test US LNG exporters mettle in the coming years.

It seems, at least in the short term, that the stars may be aligned for the USA as it pursues growth in LNG exports. "LNG is going to be very important to North America overall and the United States in particular," says John Baguley, Chief Operating Officer LNG Limited (LNGL), which is pursuing export terminal projects in Louisiana and Nova Scotia. "Even more so, U.S. LNG is going to be extremely important to the world energy market."[22] Calling the USA a "stable, long-term, reliable" supplier of highly competitively priced LNG, Baguley said that it enjoys a unique position among LNG-exporting countries. "It is not possible today to identify another place in the world that provides this critical combination of price and certainty."[23]

American entrepreneurs are specialists in squeezing unnecessary costs and inefficiencies out of a business process. One area where this is already occurring involves the global supply chain. I am fortunate to spend a lot of time in Panama and Egypt. Over the past many years, to get a first-hand sense of the dramatic expansions occurring around each of their canals, I've had many discussions with senior officials in both countries. I've come to the conclusion that there is a healthy competition stirring between the two, and, ultimately, US LNG exporters will benefit.

With US LNG exports rising, both locations are battling for that traffic from America. The newly expanded Panama Canal is now the shortest route for moving

---

[21] Ibid.
[22] Matthew V. Veazey "Views from the Crest of LNG's Second Wave: LNGL's John Baguley" *Rigzone.com* Nov 2, 2017 https://www.rigzone.com/news/views_from_the_crest_of_lngs_second_wave_lngls_john_baguley-02-nov-2017-152322-article/. Accessed January 28, 2018.
[23] Ibid.

LNG from the Gulf of Mexico to North Asia. For example, the distance from the US Gulf to Japan will be around 9,214 nautical miles, compared with 14,570 nautical miles via the Suez Canal. Assuming a speed of 19.5 knots, the reduced distance can result in savings of around 22 days on a round trip voyage from Panama. Suez is not sitting still, however. In February of 2017, the Egyptians announced an increased discount for LNG carriers, lowering rates for the first time since 1994. It is clear both locations are doing things that will enhance global trade and supply chain facilitation for decades to come. Competition between the two canals will give American LNG exporters a cost-advantage over the competition. While there are no guarantees that the future pricing of US LNG exports will remain favorable, international competitors would be well served not to ignore the ability of American businesspeople to successfully adapt, improvise, and overcome.

Geopolitical Implications of America's Shale Energy Revolution

The geopolitical implications stemming from America's energy dominance are numerous and profound. To detail them all here would require more pages than the publisher has allowed. From a big picture view, America's ability to influence geopolitics using its newfound energy prowess will only grow in the future—if the US so chooses. In July 2017, President Donald J. Trump stood in front of the Warsaw Uprising Monument in Warsaw's Krasiński Square and announced, "America stands ready to help Poland and other European nations diversify their energy supplies, so that you can never be held hostage to a single supplier." The symbolism of the moment—at a place that embodies revolt—was only overshadowed by the power of the message to Poland, the rest of Europe, Russia, and the world. The American President was clear that his nation would use its newfound energy prowess to realign and redefine its relationships with nations.

Poland's critical importance to long-term American interests cannot be underestimated. It is tied directly to America's national security. The overall objective of American foreign policy is to prohibit the rise of any single nation that can dominate the Eurasian landmass. The population of Eurasia is more than 5 billion. The Western Hemisphere, which is dominated by the US, has a little more than 1 billion people. A nation that can dominate Eurasia is the only real threat to American dominance and empire. America possesses the greatest naval power in human history. Naval supremacy assures that the U.S can never be threatened with invasion. Only a dominant nation on the Eurasian land mass could pose a direct challenge to American naval preeminence and, ultimately, the homeland. As a result, American foreign policy conducts itself with a fixed eye to assuring a balance of power around the world, particularly in Eurasia. In other words, the US works to ensure that no one nation becomes too strong or too weak. A major nation in Eurasia that becomes too strong, such as the Soviet Union attempted, could put the US at risk. Hence America's establishment and commitment to NATO during the Cold War.

At the same time, weakened nations allow for stronger nations to gain from that weakness. This is currently what is happening in Europe as Germany and Russia seek to build a stronger alliance across Eurasia, with German machinery and know-how going east, and Russian energy moving west. Poland's strategic location right in the middle of these two nations allows the US to check this growing German/Russian alliance. American energy sales to Poland will inexorably bind the two for decades to come, eliminating Poland's dependence on Russia energy imports and German capital investment. It can be argued that Poland is now undergoing what Israel and South Korea have already experienced: the construction of a strategic relationship with the US Rooted in shared common interests and fuelled by American energy, Poland seems positioned to become America's critical ally in Central Europe for decades to come. This would not have been possible were it not for America's shale energy revolution. The same is happening with Japan, a key American ally in East Asia. As China seeks to project power beyond its borders, Japan, increasingly importing American shale energy, will serve as the blocker to any Chinese ambitions. Of course, increased Japanese need for US energy exports will allow America to make sure that Japan doesn't get too strong either.

A Middle East Case Study: Saudi Arabia

While the USA had become the world's largest overall energy producer by 2015, Saudi Arabia remained the global leader in oil production. That changed in early 2018, when the International Energy Agency announced that US crude oil output was likely to climb to 10.4 million barrels per day, which would top the high set in 1970. Saudi Arabia had been the world's leading oil producer since for more than 5 decades. The Kingdom produces a little under ten million barrels a day, and has said in the past it can produce up to 12 million, although it has never pumped more than 10.5 million.[24] While the IEA announcement in January 2018 received big headlines and had many wondering how the USA/Saudi relationship would change, it was clear that massive shifts were already well underway for a number of years.

Following the 1973 oil embargo and economic shock caused by the Kingdom's response to the West's support of Israel in its war with Egypt, the relationship between the two nations was always marked with tension. Americans were more than happy to sell hundreds of billions of dollars in military hardware to the Saudis. Yet, real concerns remained that, if given the right set of circumstances, the Saudis would repeat the actions of the past. The message from Riyadh to Washington was both subtle and clear: "You may be the world's superpower, yet if you challenge our interests, there will be hell to pay. Much of the oil you so desperately need to make your Empire possible is in our hands, not yours." This was a lesson that was not forgotten by American leaders for nearly two generations.

The terror attacks of September 11, 2001 illustrated how America had bent to Saudi oil dominance over the years. Fifteen of the nineteen hijackers on that fateful day were Saudi nationals. Osama Bin Laden, the leader of Al-Qaeda, was a Saudi.

---

[24] Christopher Alessi and Alison Sider "U.S. to Topple Saudis in Oil Output" *Wall Street Journal* Janaury 20-12, 2018, p. A1.

It was suspected, and later confirmed, that much of the financing of the operation had originated in the Kingdom.

A mere 11 days after the attacks, while fires still smoldered at Ground Zero and the Pentagon, President George W. Bush signed the Air Transportation Safety and System Stability Act into law. In the House the vote was 356-54. In the Senate it was 96-1. While much attention was paid to the huge bailout, the Federal Government gave the airline industry ultimately more than $2 billion—a lesser but still critical part of the bill remained out of the public discussion. This involved potential litigation on behalf of the victims of the attack.[25]

A fund was established under the law that enabled governmental compensation to a victim's family if "the claimant waives the right to file a civil action (or to be a party to an action) in any Federal or State court for damages sustained as a result of the terrorist-related aircraft crashes of September 11, 2001."[26] This meant that if you agreed not to sue anyone, including the airlines, security companies, or foreign actors for their role in 9/11, the Federal Government would compensate you for the loss of your loved one. Conversely, if you wanted to hold someone accountable for his or her death and enter the legal system, you'd get nothing from the compensation fund.

While the vast majority of victims' families agreed to the stipulation, signed away their right to sue, and took the compensation funds, 96 families opted out. Many of them later sued the nation of Saudi Arabia and members of the royal family for their actions surrounding the 9/11 plot. Always sensitive to the Saudi response, the US government pushed back against the victims' families. On May 29, 2009, the President's top lawyer before the Supreme Court, Solicitor General Elena Kagan, filed a brief arguing that it would be "unwarranted" for the Supreme Court to even hear cases brought by the 9/11 families charging that five Saudi princes knowingly and intentionally provided financial support to Al Qaeda waging war on America. By urging the high court to not review lower court decisions dismissing these cases, the Obama Administration took the side of the Saudi princes over the family members and survivors of the 9/11 attacks seeking justice and accountability in US courts. The Saudis, it seemed, were insulated.

Still the families fought on. Working tirelessly on Capitol Hill, they lobbied members of both parties to get legislation passed that would assure them of their ability to get a fair hearing. Introduced in the Senate as S. 2040 by John Cornyn (R-TX) on September 16, 2015, it passed the Senate on May 17, 2016 and the House on September 9. However, President Barack Obama vetoed it on September 23. Nevertheless, The Justice Against Sponsors of Terrorism Act (JASTA) became law when Democrats and Republicans on Capitol Hill came together to override the veto. The Senate vote was 97-1. The House vote a few hours later was 348-77, with 123 Democrats rebuffing the President. The victims' families deserve the bulk of

---

[25] Andrew R. Thomas *Aviation Insecurity: The New Challenges of Air Travel* (Prometheus, 2003) p. 73.

[26] H.R.2926 - *Air Transportation Safety and System Stabilization Act* 107th Congress (2001-2002) https://www.congress.gov/bill/107th-congress/house-bill/2926. Accessed January 22, 2018

the credit for keeping the issue alive and never backing down. One wonders if the emergence of America's shale energy revolution didn't also play a critical role.

Left with no real options, the Saudis mustered a token threat to sell up to $750 billion in US Treasury securities and other US assets if the bill passed. It became clear to everyone in Washington that the Saudis had been effectively marginalized. A new reality was emerging for the world to see: Due to America's rising energy power, major oil-producing nations like Saudi Arabia could no longer take hostages and threaten the economic well-being of the American—and global—economies. Going forward, America will have a far greater degree of flexibility when it comes to managing relationships with the nations of the world than anytime in the recent past. The US will have more opportunity to "pick and choose" what it decides to do and where, and with whom. As real concerns over domestic energy security have subsided, the natural tendencies of American foreign policy can now unfold without a lot of obstacles in the way.

America's Foreign Policy Realignment and Shale Energy

So what forms the natural tendencies of American foreign policy? Is it the isolation-ism of the late nineteenth and early twentieth centuries? Is it the Wilsonian view of American engagement in the twentieth century that led to the creation of the Bretton Woods System? Is it a desire on the part of elites like Henry Luce to spread American ideals around the world? Or, is it the goal to enrich American firms and investors by tapping into new markets around the world? As with any complicated question, there are many elements that constitute the answer. Nevertheless, it is clear that the Post-World War II international system is beginning to wind down. It will not end tomorrow or next year or even within the next decade. Yet, the pullback of the United States from the guarantees that have underpinned the system is already underway.

Many might think America's floundering commitment is the result of Donald Trump's election in November 2016. This is too narrowly focused. Most recently, the American people have chosen three Presidents who campaigned on disentan-gling the U.S. from its post-World War II assurances. America's withdrawal from its status as the world's singular superpower began in earnest as the country's shale energy revolution took off. Barack Obama's notion of America "leading from behind" became a fundamental pillar of his second administration's foreign policy. As a candidate and President, Obama railed against US entanglements and nation building. Even George W. Bush, who might be best remembered for leading the adventures into Iraq, Afghanistan, and beyond, was elected in 2000 on a platform of disengagement from the rest of the world. The 9/11 attacks radically changed Bush's views, and likely would have altered Al Gore's as well had he been President. Of course, Bush was also confronted with the very serious threat of America's growing dependency on foreign sources of energy to sustain the global system it created. For Obama, once American shale energy entered into the equation, he was able to return to his instincts and seek to limit America's involvement in foreign affairs. If any-thing, Trump's election was a logical progression of America's re-evaluation of

Bretton Woods in the past decade fostered by the shale energy revolution. Around the world, flashpoints are moving towards full-blown conflicts that America looks eager to avoid.

A fundamental reality of the Bretton Woods commitments that the USA laid out to the allies—and then everyone else—is the lack of involvement of the American people in its creation. The Bretton Woods Conference was held in July 1944, 4 months before a Presidential election and a month after the Allied landings at D-Day. The attention of the American people and many of their elected representatives was clearly elsewhere. Remembering that Woodrow Wilson's appeal to the US Senate for its approval of the League of Nations after World War I was rejected, the Roosevelt Administration took a far different course. When given its chance during World War II to create "The American Century," the Roosevelt Administration didn't bother with constitutional requirements under Article I and ignored Congress' sole authority to approve foreign treaties and agreements. Instead, they just did it. Over time, the reality of Bretton Woods melded into a kind of *fait accompli*, where America was the creator and sustainer of the new international system. No one really challenged the creation of Bretton Woods because no one—except for a few key elites—was even aware that it had been created in the first place. By the time the War ended and people learned of its existence, Bretton Woods was already way down the road.

Foreign policy—and support for the Bretton Woods system—remained the purview of a small American elite across governmental agencies, academe, industry, and the military for generations. These unelected folks guided incoming Presidents in the "ways of the world"—and maintained consensus that the Bretton Woods system must always be supported. The only American presidents with any kind of international relations experience after World War II were Dwight Eisenhower and George H.W. Bush, both of whom deeply supported the Bretton Woods system and America's role in maintaining it. The others leaned heavily on entrenched foreign policy elites in the Pentagon, State Department, CIA, multinational corporations, and universities for guidance and direction.

One of the biggest stories that the media and other so-called analysts have missed in recent years is the challenge to the Bretton Woods system that has been occurring with the United States. Paradoxically, the one nation that has come up short in enjoying the tremendous benefits of the American-led Bretton Woods system is the United States itself. The USA is overwhelmingly a domestic-focused economy, and always has been. Today, only about 15% of all US GDP is tied to international trade, with around half of that energy imports, which are declining fast. This is in alignment with historical trends over the past 150 years. As the shale revolution continues to expand, American energy imports and dependence on foreign players will continue to decrease in coming years.

Moreover, concerns about burgeoning entitlement costs as the baby boomers continue to exit the workplace find more and more Americans rightly worried about ballooning deficits and obligations to their fellow citizens - and themselves. Trade agreements that were positioned to the American people as fundamental to continued prosperity began to lose credibility with voters of all stripes as factories shuttered and millions of jobs were outsourced overseas. The major party candidates in

2016—Trump and Hilary Clinton—both rejected America joining the Trans Pacific Partnership, which had taken over a decade to negotiate and was birthed in the USA! In short, Americans across the political spectrum are asking: "What is our return-on-investment for the trillions we have spent to build and maintain the global capitalist system?" Answers are hard to find. There are, of course, domestic benefits to America's engagement with the global economy, yet they are not as profound as many believe; and, quite difficult to articulate for the supporters of globalization.

A New World Disorder?

As America withdraws from the same global system it created in 1944, the consequences to the USA will be almost negligible. Safely ensconced in its continental "dominion from sea to sea," the USA will enjoy the fruits of its seemingly endless bounty without major disruption or threat. Domestic shale energy will only accelerate America's withdrawal. Meanwhile, the rest of the world will return to "normal." Minus the guarantees of the American security blanket, ethnic and regional antipathies will flare once again. Military spending will continue to balloon. Wars and rumors of wars amongst major nations will return. Large powers will bang into each other as they scour the world for ever-scarcer resources and markets. Business costs will rise and friction will reign. People outside the United States viscerally know this and it scares them to death. This seems to be one of the primary reasons so much of the world hates Donald Trump. He has given a voice and a face to their worst fear: a world where America can no longer be counted on.

This does not mean, however, that Americans will refrain from exploring global business opportunities. Nor does it signify that American foreign policy will abandon international pursuits. American corporations will still look to sell consumer goods, aircraft, arms and weapons, and energy to foreign markets where profits can be made. US foreign policy will advance these commercial interests, as it always has. At the highest strategic level, America will pursue a balance of power in Eurasia. Poland, for example, will become a stronger and stronger ally. Yet, what is being altered—because of America's shale energy revolution—is the level of intensity that has marked American global involvement since the creation of Bretton Woods. US energy ascendancy will foster a level of American disengagement in global affairs that the Nation—and the world—has not seen in decades. In short, American global activity will be less aggressive and less certain. Instead, American power will be increasingly harnessed to foster development at home—rather than abroad. "America First" will become more and more the focus of US politics. America's shale energy revolution makes all this possible.

In the South China Sea, concerns over Chinese territorial expansion and North Korea's nuclear program have Japan, in particular, very worried about America's continued guarantees of peace and stability in the region. It should come as no surprise that the first foreign visitor to Trump Tower after the November 2016 election was Prime Minister Abe of Japan. Further, the nations of the region, being so dependent on international shipping to transport their energy needs, are developing their own naval capabilities to assure the flow of imports and exports.

As Russia reintroduced major war into Eurasia, first in 2008 with its invasion of Georgia, and later with its invasion of Ukraine in 2014, followed by the shoot-down of a commercial airliner in 2016, Bush and Obama did almost nothing. Trump has been just recalcitrant to act since taking office. As Russia continues to wear down the Ukrainian Army, it seems just a matter of time before Russia tanks move on Kiev: a stated goal of the Putin regime for more than a decade. Further, the rising Russian threat posed to other nations including Belarus and Moldova, and the Baltics has Europe on high alert. Concerned about America's waning commitment to the continent's security, military spending is way up.

In the Middle East, a cold war between Iran and Saudi Arabia is getting hot very quickly. Proxy wars in Syria, Iraq, and Yemen between the two regional powers have the real potential to become a direct confrontation. The arms race is building, as both nations are spending billions to acquire the latest in offensive and defensive hardware. Where is America in all this? Strangely detached and disinterested.

Much of what has been presented here lies outside of the headlines from the daily news and talking heads. To best understand the world for what it is and might be, the trend lines are what matter most. The picture of the business and geopolitical implications of America's shale energy painted here is, in fact, two-sided. On one side of the canvas, there are tremendous benefits for American businesses, consumers, and innovators. On the other side, there exist real grave concerns that America's ultimate exit from Bretton Woods—facilitated by energy security—is already leaving many in a lurch. It seems the pause button of the last 80-plus years is now being released and a "return to history" is unfolding right before our eyes.

Acknowledgments

A book is always more than the efforts and enthusiasm of the author. This book would not have been possible without Bob Schmidt. My work with Bob as part of the relationship between the University of Akron and MAGNET was the original spark. Bob's friendship, unwavering support, and firm desire to help our students are hallmarks of his true character.

Early and ongoing conversations with Chris Hensley, Paul Horbaly, Pat D'Andrea, Paul Boulier, Bill Baker, Paul Thomarios, and James Halloran convinced me that a book like this could be of value. They each graciously volunteered to help me learn- and patiently listened to my thoughts and ideas.

My long-time editors at Springer—Nitza Jones-Sepulveda and Nick Phillipson—have supported my writing and research adventures for years; and, always work so hard to make them even better. Nick, that semicolon was for you. Finally, it is because of Jackie, Paul Bryan, and Alana that I do what I do.

Any errors, omissions, or mistakes are mine, and mine alone.

© The Author(s), under exclusive licence to Springer International Publishing AG,   53
part of Springer Nature 2018
A. R. Thomas, *American Shale Energy and the Global Economy,* SpringerBriefs
in Business, https://doi.org/10.1007/978-3-319-89306-8

Printed by Printforce, the Netherlands